LOVE, Joy & PEACE

A WORD*Girls* Collective

A WORD*Girls* Collective

Foreword by WordGirls Founder, Kathy Carlton Willis

LOVE, Joy & PEACE

A 12-Week Devotional to
Shine the Light on God's Word

3G Books

Love, Joy & Peace ©2024 by Kathy Carlton Willis
www.kathycarltonwillis.com
ISBN 979-8-9888761-1-3
Published by 3G Books, Tyler, TX 75703

All rights reserved. No part of this book may be reproduced, stored in a retrieval system, or transmitted in any form or by any means—electronic, mechanical, photocopy, recording, or otherwise—without written permission of the publisher, except for brief quotations in printed reviews.

Scripture quotations marked NLT are taken from the Holy Bible, New Living Translation, copyright © 1996, 2004, 2015 by Tyndale House Foundation. Used by permission of Tyndale House Publishers, Inc., Carol Stream, Illinois 60188. All rights reserved.

Scripture quotations marked ESV are from The Holy Bible, English Standard Version. ESV® Text Edition: 2016. Copyright © 2001 by Crossway Bibles, a publishing ministry of Good News Publishers.

Scripture quotations marked AMP are taken from the Amplified® Bible, Copyright © 2015 by The Lockman Foundation. La Habra, CA 90631. All rights reserved. Used by permission. www.Lockman.org

Scripture quotations marked MSG are taken from *THE MESSAGE*, copyright © 1993, 2002, 2018 by Eugene H. Peterson. Used by permission of NavPress. All rights reserved. Represented by Tyndale House Publishers, Inc.

Scriptures marked NKJV are taken from the New King James Version®. Copyright © 1982 by Thomas Nelson. Used by permission. All rights reserved.

Copyedited by Kathy Carlton Willis

Editing, Interior, and Cover Design by Michelle Rayburn
www.missionandmedia.com

Contents

Foreword ix
About WordGirls. xi
Shine Bright Star *Carolyn Gaston*. xv

LOVE

Bubble Bath at Epiphany's *Lisa-Anne Wooldridge* 3
A Meltdown and a Lesson *Missy Eversole* 5
Opening My Heart *Diana Leagh Matthews*. 7
One Hundred Percent Love *Carolyn Gaston* 9
I See You *Sandy Lipsky* 11
A Friend in the Battles *Betty Predmore* 13
He "Hearts" Me *Susan Stitch* 15
Love Silenced the Wolves *Charlaine Martin* 17
Love That Keeps Us Together *Joni Topper* 19
God's Love Outshines Despair *Natasha Lynn Daniels* . . . 21
Nothing Shall Separate *Susanne Moore*. 23
The Choir Director's Miracle *Beth Jennings Patch* 25
The Gospel Is Love *Pattie Reitz* 27
I Love You More *Stacy Sanchez*. 29
No Regrets *Joanie Shawhan* 31
God's Appointment *Joanie Shawhan* 33
Love Ain't So Crazy *Hally J. Wells*. 35
Finding Comfort In the Chaos *Beth Jennings Patch* 37

v

From Fear to Comfort *Missy Eversole* 39
The One Tree *Lisa-Anne Wooldridge* 41
That's Mine! *Sally Ferguson* 43
This Moment Is Proof *Robin Steinweg* 45
Love the Name *Sandy Lipsky* 47
Viv's Mission of Love *Denise Margaret Ackerman* 49
Hope for Tomorrow *Joanie Shawhan* 51
Safe in God's Love *Pattie Reitz* 53
The God Who Bends Down *Becki James* 55
Borrowed Fruit *Sandy Lipsky* 57
Lessons from the Fall *Janice Metot* 59
Secure in Love *Becki James* 61

JOY

All Kinds of Joy *Robin Steinweg* 65
How Do I Get That Joy? *Joni Topper* 67
A Two-Dollar Bill and Ice Cream *Charlaine Martin* 69
I Will Joy *Robin Steinweg* 71
Surprised by Joy *Sandy Lipsky* 73
It's Snow Problem, Mom! *Lisa-Anne Wooldridge* 75
Dawn Is Breaking *Diana Leagh Matthews* 77
Glorious, Inexpressible Joy *Dawn Wilson* 79
The Endurance of Joy *Kathy Carlton Willis* 81
Rain Dance *Lisa-Anne Wooldridge* 83
The Wonder of the Sunrise *Susan Stitch* 85
A Heavenly Rejoicing *Susanne Moore* 87
Joy from the Graveyard *Beth Jennings Patch* 89

Jesus and the Golden Arches *Stacy Sanchez* 91
Just Hold Him Tight *Beth Jennings Patch* 93
Artesian Well *Robin Steinweg*. 95
Joy in the Face of Sorrow *Joni Topper*. 97
On the Trail to Joy *Beth Kirkpatrick* 99
The Journey *Sally Ferguson* 101
No Sing, Mama! *Missy Eversole*. 103
A Tranquil Heart of Joy *Denise Margaret Ackerman* 105
Heart Cushions *Mindy Cantrell* 107
Are You Listening? *Carolyn Gaston* 109
Gathering the Harvest of Joy *Edna Earney* 111
God Delights in Me *Robin Steinweg*. 113
Restore My Joy *Pattie Reitz*. 115
Spilling Over with Joy *Denise Margaret Ackerman*. 117
Front Porch Storytelling *Lisa-Anne Wooldridge* 119

PEACE

Peace Chips *Sandy Lipsky* 123
Learning to Live Peaceably *Betty Predmore* 125
Learning to Love Peace *Kathy Carlton Willis* 127
Just Pray *Susan Stitch* 129
Facets of Friendship *Joanie Shawhan*. 131
Heaven's Morning Light *Becki James* 133
Nunc Dimittis *Beth Kirkpatrick*. 135
Did You Say Peas or Peace? *Joni Topper*. 137
The Fringe of His Coat *Mary Harker* 139
Winds of Peace *Becki James* 141

Our Miracle-Working Warrior *Edna Earney* 143
Not Without You *Joni Topper* 145
Finding Peace and Purpose *Mary Harker* 147
Finding True Peace *Natasha Lynn Daniels* 149
The Trail of Heart's Ease *Lisa-Anne Wooldridge* 151
Peace on Earth *Diana Leagh Matthews*. 153
Trouble Sleeping? *Robin Steinweg*. 155
An Open Microphone of Peace *Dixie McLeod* 157
Promised Prayer *Susan Stitch* 159
God Calms the Storm *Susanne Moore*. 161
Restoring Peace and Love *Missy Eversole* 163
Will You Qualify? *Beth Jennings Patch* 165
The Peace-Piece Conundrum *Hally J. Wells*. 167
Battling for Peace *Robin Steinweg*. 169
Road Trip *Sally Ferguson*. 171
With Peace as My Purpose *Edna Earney*. 173
Got You Covered *Mary Harker*. 175
Who Wears the White Hat? *Edna Earney* 177
Peace Brings Life and Health *Carolyn Gaston*. 179
Peace in God's Presence *Becki James*. 181
Calm Instead of Chaos *Kathy Carlton Willis*. 183

Our Contributors 185
Notes 198
Acknowledgments 199
WordGirls Collective Books 201

A Foreword by Our Founder

I've always loved the vintage VW buses and other vans from that era. They make me think of road trips. I've been on literal road trips with several of the WordGirls. Oh, the stories we could tell! And symbolically, all of the WordGirls have been on a road trip with God, with each other, and with you as our readers. There's a trend these days called "van life," and I'm going to suggest there is a spiritual version of that. A hymn used the term "just passing through."[1] Our destination isn't in this world but the next.

Some have different views of the hippie mindset. Yes, there was a godless component. We're not here to take you down that road. But God and his Word started the trend when it comes to love, joy, and peace. And maybe there's nothing wrong with a little fun along the way—no drugs needed for that kind of psychedelic colors and bell-bottom pants!

As the editor of this devotional and the founder of Word-Girls, I have a special affinity for these spiritual attributes. I've even written a couple of Bible studies on the terms. So, it comes as no surprise to me that we're also exploring the ideas of love, joy, and peace with this devotional. Reading what the others have written on the subject makes my heart grin big.

We pray these words will lead you on your own road trip toward love, joy, and peace.

On the road trip with you,

Kathy Carlton Willis, WordGirls Founder and God's Grin Gal

About WordGirls

Ten years ago (2014), I had a brainchild to start a group to coach fun, faith-filled women who were serious about the writing life. I served on faculty at national writer's conferences and realized attendees remained stuck in the writing process. They were often overwhelmed by the conference material and didn't know how to apply it to their writing lives. I'd see them return year after year with their projects showing little progress. They needed a group to keep them accountable and a coach to help them figure out their next steps.

WordGirls is a special sisterhood of writing support for women who write from a biblical worldview (whether for the faith market or general market). We propel writers to the next level—regardless of where they are today.

Here's an overview of our exclusive WordGirls benefits:

1. Once-per-year individual phone coaching to personalize your advancement as a writer and/or speaker.
2. Private Facebook group to interact, brainstorm, pray for each other, share ideas, ask questions, etc.
3. Monthly topics to help you grow as a writer. To enhance your learning, we will cover the topics through Facebook group discussions and Zoom live sessions (recorded for you to watch later if you can't make it live).
4. The Blessing Seat think tanks during our video meetings (more details below).

5. Downloadable PDFs offer extra training in the form of tutorials.

6. Weekly study hall. We designate Fridays to work on projects we call our B.I.C. time (butt in chair). Study hall provides added accountability. (If you can't make it, we cheer you on whenever you designate your B.I.C. time.)

7. Periodic challenges. Some challenges are month-long, and others last a season. These challenges will stretch you without overwhelming you. They are guaranteed to increase productivity if you participate. (Participation is not required to be a member.)

8. Digital membership badge to post on your website or social media page.

9. Reduced rates for events and for-fee materials. We have online retreats and WordGirls@Home intensives. We offer WordGirls Getaways as circumstances allow.

10. Opportunity to submit writing for our WordGirls publications.

11. Additional services when you hire our coach for a reduced hourly rate only available to members.

AROUND-THE-CLOCK B.I.C. RELAY

We host two twenty-four-hour B.I.C. relays a year. Members commit to writing for at least one hour. Some do more, and some time slots have two members, but added together, we work around the clock. We imagine we are on a relay race, passing the baton to the writer taking over the next time slot. As we pass the baton, we pray for them. Many participants use the team roster as a prayer list and pray for everyone by name. We send prayer notes and posts to each other to encourage and cheer on. It is quite uplifting! Members say their productivity levels surge during our special relays—thanks to the extra inspiration and motivation.

BOOKS

In 2020, WordGirls created a group-funded compilation book that released in March 2021: *Wit, Whimsy & Wisdom*. Our second book released in November 2021: *Snapshots of Hope & Heart*. While the first two books are devotionals, our third and fourth books are collections of essays. *Live & Learn: Unexpected Lessons from God's Classroom* released in 2022, and we had a fun and meaningful virtual book club with readers going through the book together.

In 2023, we published *Sage, Salt & Sunshine: Women Inspiring Women with Insight, Truth, Light & Joy*. With two cups on the cover, it's the perfect inspiration for a women's tea or book club group. It celebrates the positive influence other women have as they pour into us. Now, it's our turn to pour into others.

Who may submit to WordGirls writing projects? Anyone who is a member at some time during the same calendar year as the call for submissions or attended a WordGirls intensive, getaway, or retreat during that year.

THE BLESSING SEAT

Some mastermind groups have an interactive process called the hot seat. A member shares their project with the group and receives input and brainstorming, much like a think tank. We decided the term "hot seat" made it sound like a high-pressure inquisition! So, our group offers a grace-filled version of a think tank called *The Blessing Seat*. We assist members in getting their questions answered and their projects propelled to the next stage.

SIZE OF GROUP

To keep the group intimate, we grant a limited number of memberships. We only have open enrollment twice per year: in January (for a February to January membership period) and in July (for an August to July membership period). You'll find a registration form at kathycarltonwillis.com/wordgirls. If you have questions, email kathy@kathycarltonwillis.com.

We also open up the online and in-person retreats to non-members, so keep an eye on the website for details of upcoming events.

Shine, Bright Star

by Carolyn Gaston

Shine, bright star; have mercy on me.
Please let this long night end.
Open my eyes and help me see.
You're my Savior and my friend.

Shine, bright star; lead me to grace.
This heaviness hurts my heart.
I seek your presence; I seek your face.
I need a clear, new start.

Shine, bright star; permeate me with peace.
Remove this smothering shadow.
I need you, God, to give me strength.
I need hope for tomorrow.

Shine, bright star of eternal love.
Let your righteousness shine like the dawn.
Send your peace and joy from above.
Help me sing a sweet, new song.

Shine, bright star of everlasting light.
Your kindness draws me to you.
I've been frozen in this fight,
But I know you'll pull me through.

Shine, bright star of Bethlehem,
Like the night when Christ was born.
You can heal this pain within.
You're mighty to transform.

Shine, bright star of Christmastime.
Bring comfort to my soul.
Reign in my heart; bring peace of mind.
I give you full control.

Shine, bright star. O shine, bright star.
The wait has been so hard.
Shine bright star. O shine, bright star.
For I do trust you, Lord.

Love

Bubble Bath at Epiphany's

by Lisa-Anne Wooldridge

We know how much God loves us, and we have put our trust in his love. God is love, and all who live in love live in God, and God lives in them.

1 JOHN 4:16 (NLT)

I SIGHED AND SANK deeper into the warm, fragrant water that filled my clawfoot tub. *What bliss!* The bubbles were thick, full of flower petals, and lit by mini glowsticks beneath the surface. Scented candles and essential oils made me feel like I was in the fairy garden of my dreams.

"I love you. I want you to know that."

I knew my husband loved me, but it was clear he wanted me to understand something even deeper about his love and care for me. He's always been the best person to demonstrate God's love to me too. I closed my eyes and relaxed, determined to enjoy what he'd prepared for me.

My brain had other ideas.

The lyrics to "I Want to Know What Love Is" began to play in my mind. I turned the song into a prayer, though, and told God I wanted him to show me.

I'll never be able to adequately explain what happened next. A tidal wave of memories washed over me, bringing a surge of raw emotion. Snippets of songs, sermons, and conversations. Memories of people dear to my heart. Thoughts of my encounters with

God from childhood onward. I was overwhelmed for a minute, but then I laughed. I imagined myself like a game-show contestant in a glass booth filled with flying dollars—I was trying to grab and hold onto as much of that treasure as I could before the clock ran out. That's when it hit me.

God *is* love.

I didn't need to scramble for understanding. Love isn't going anywhere. Love will never fail me, leave me, forget me, or even look sideways at me. In love, I live and move and have my being. I am surrounded by love. Love wakes me up in the morning and sings me to sleep at night. Love dreamed me up, and love gives me life.

It's easier for me to recognize love now. That gush of affection that rushes out of me for the person in my path, that's love. That desire to draw someone in and wrap my arms around them, that's love. Love is a wonderful verb, and it's the ultimate noun. Love is my favorite person, my happiest place, my most cherished possession. Love lives in us. We live in love.

> Loving Father, help me know and believe the love you have for us. Let me soak in your love and carry the fragrance of your presence everywhere I go. Thank you for giving me a lifetime to learn what love is and an eternity to explore the depths of your heart.

A Meltdown and a Lesson

by Missy Eversole

Do not love the world or the things in the world. If anyone loves the world, the love of the Father is not in him.

1 JOHN 2:15 (ESV)

HAVE YOU EVER had a meltdown? I'm talking about a foot-stomping, arms-flailing, screaming-at-the-top-of-your-lungs meltdown?

I have, and I was in the pick-up line at my son's school in front of everyone. It wasn't my finest parenting moment.

At that time in my life, I was physically tired, emotionally drained, and spiritually depleted. The word *boundary* was not in my vocabulary, so when asked to do something, I did it. I wanted to look like a dependable, faithful woman everyone could count on.

Because of this, my family suffered. My calendar was filled to the max, and the stress of it all took a toll on me.

Worst of all, I was going through the motions in my relationship with Jesus. I showed up for church, filled in the blanks for the women's Bible study book, and that was it. I did the bare minimum. Lukewarm in my faith—the fire I once had for Jesus was almost extinguished.

My meltdown in the parking lot was a wake-up call. I was loving the world by getting wrapped up in people-pleasing and not God.

While I chased society's definition of success and acceptance, I lost sight of my identity in Jesus. The more I tried to strive for perfection, the further I drifted from the warmth of God's love.

So, I took a step back. I started to say no to things that would cause me additional stress. I rediscovered the joy of a genuine relationship with Jesus. As I let go of the high expectations I placed on myself, I found rest in the arms of a loving Savior.

My family no longer had a stressed-out wife and a stretched-thin mom. Instead, they found a woman who, though imperfect, was rooted in the unchanging love of Christ.

True rest and fulfillment are not found in the world but in surrendering to the boundless love of our heavenly Father.

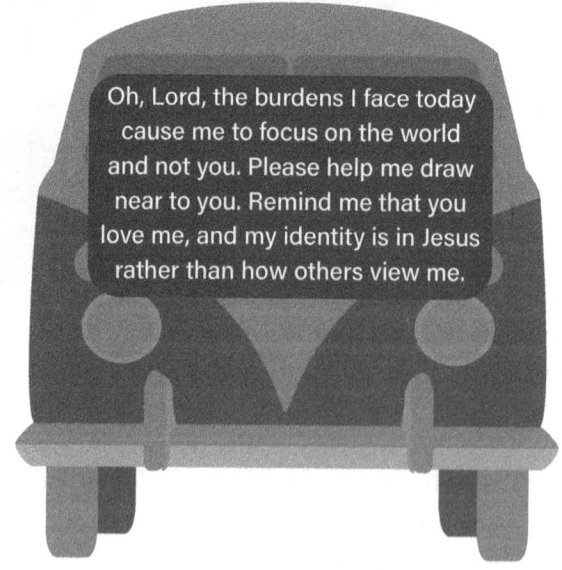

Oh, Lord, the burdens I face today cause me to focus on the world and not you. Please help me draw near to you. Remind me that you love me, and my identity is in Jesus rather than how others view me.

Opening My Heart

by Diana Leagh Matthews

We love because he first loved us.

1 JOHN 4:19 (ESV)

ALL ALONE. LONELINESS ran rampant in my life and heart. Abusive relationships made it difficult for me to trust others. Long work hours and caregiving duties kept me busy and exhausted. I cried out to the Lord, "Will it always be this way?"

I tried to put on a good front, but each year, the cloak of loneliness grew tighter and heavier around me.

More than once, I perused the animal shelters, searching and wishing for a companion, but with my long hours away from home, I knew it wouldn't be fair to an animal.

Then life reset itself. My job changed. I moved. My grandmother died.

One evening, I prayed, "Lord, just send me someone to love who will love me in return." I didn't know who or what I was praying for, only that I couldn't go on all alone any longer.

Apparently, the Lord had been waiting for me to ask because in less than two weeks, a co-worker shared they needed to re-home one of their dogs. The moment I saw his picture, I was smitten. Plus, he was exactly what I needed. Small and hypoallergenic.

Two days later, I met Bentley, a ten-pound Maltese mix, and he came directly to me. No barking or whimpering. Just snuggled in my arms as if he belonged there. Love exploded through my heart.

Each day, I find something new to enjoy and love about him. Walks. Ball chasing. Tug of war. Belly rubs. Dancing together. Going for rides. Reading to him. But our favorite times are always the early morning and late night snuggles.

Bentley provides the companionship I crave, and because of him, I've tried activities—such as walking at various parks or eating outdoors—I would not have tried otherwise. He's become the child I always longed for and never had.

Sometimes, to expel loneliness we must be willing to open our hearts and allow others to love us in return. And more than the love found on earth through humans and animals, we can always tune in to the love of the Father, knowing that he loved us first.

Is there someone or something you need to open your heart to today?

Lord, you did not create us to be alone. Thank you for giving me others to love and who love me in return. Help me remember that while it's wonderful to have family and fur babies, you are the only one who completely knows my needs and can fill my heart.

One Hundred Percent Love

by Carolyn Gaston

Let me hear in the morning of your steadfast love, for in you I trust.

PSALM 143:8 (ESV)

PULLING ONE PRETTY petal at a time from the delicate daisy, I chanted over and over, "He loves me. He loves me not." I wanted to know if that cute fourth-grade boy liked me. Maybe he did—maybe he didn't.

Do you remember playing this silly game? There was only a 50 percent chance that we would get the answer we wanted. Human love can be just that uncertain and risky. But God's love, on the other hand, is always 100 percent perfect and unconditional. Every morning, I can remember this great truth, and because I believe God loves me with steadfast love, I can trust him.

To be the woman God designed me to be, I must wholeheartedly believe that he loves me unconditionally. I must not put conditions on his love. I have to relax in the assurance that God's love is perfect. I am his child, and that makes me valuable in his eyes. I know I don't deserve this love, and I know I can't earn it.

There is absolutely nothing I can do to make God love me more. So, I have to focus on his presence and his purpose and not on my performance, or I can't receive his love completely.

Sometimes I feel unworthy of God's love and let guilt and shame swallow me up and drive me away from him. That's when I have to stop, forgive myself, and ask for his mercy and grace. It's important to remember once again that his love is always unconditional and unfailing. Just like King David, I need to be reminded that God's love never changes. How am I reminded every day of this powerful promise? A raindrop? A hug from a friend? A poem? A song? If you can think of a song about God's great love at this very moment, pause and remember once again that his love is steadfast and eternal. Our Father God loves us 100 percent!

Lord, help me more fully grasp the concept of your unfailing, unconditional love. May I focus on your purpose for my life so I will not be driven by feelings of shame and unworthiness. Thank you that your love is perfect.

I See You

by Sandy Lipsky

He remembered us in our weakness. His faithful love endures forever.

PSALM 136:23 (NLT)

*F*OR SEVEN YEARS, I passed his house. My walk took me through a local neighborhood where the residents waved and stopped to chat. I knew most of the people on my route.

One afternoon, an unfamiliar man caught my attention as he shuffled down his driveway. His appearance shocked my senses. Long, gray, unkempt hair brushed against his collar. The unbuttoned shirt flapped open, exposing his protruding ribs. One hand grasped the waistband of his sweatpants while the other arm swung as if to keep his momentum moving forward.

"Hi," I blurted.

My voice stopped his motion. Feeling awkward as he stared in my direction, I kept moving.

He needs help.

The next day, I heard a siren close by. A group of neighbors huddled near an emergency vehicle as I passed the bedraggled man's home.

A week later, I bumped into one of the bystanders. She recounted how the man had fallen and gashed his head on the concrete outside.

"He's back home now. He has addictions," she whispered.

After prayer, I decided to take the stranger a loaf of homemade bread. As I crept up his driveway, I spotted a rocking chair on the porch. *I'll knock on the door and leave the bread there.*

He invited me in after a series of food drop-offs. Fear did not enter my mind. Due to his weakened state, I could have knocked him down with ease. His feet were bare and swollen. He collapsed on his couch as I scanned the layout. Quickly, I realized my inability to smell was a gift. Stacked on every surface were piles of empty liquor bottles and trash. Once I saw his need, I frequented his house for visits and to clean. We became friends. Walter*—estranged from family and isolated by addiction—had become invisible to the world.

But he was not invisible. God saw him and opened my eyes to see him too.

I stopped by Walter's house for our daily visit after being away for a holiday. In the past, when I knocked, he would shout, "Come in darlin'." But this time, there was no answer. I checked with neighbors and local hospitals before calling the police. Hours later, I received the gut-wrenching news.

I miss Walter. In my grief, I remember God loved him so much he sent him a friend. I'm glad it was me.

*Name changed.

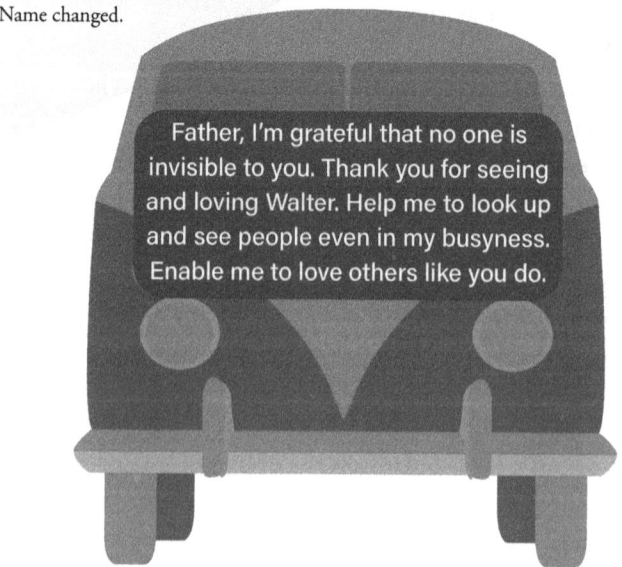

Father, I'm grateful that no one is invisible to you. Thank you for seeing and loving Walter. Help me to look up and see people even in my busyness. Enable me to love others like you do.

A Friend in the Battles

by Betty Predmore

A friend loves at all times, And a brother is born for adversity.

PROVERBS 17:17 (NKJV)

THE SKY WAS pitch black—with no moon to light the way—as my mom led my brother and me away from our home and toward safety.

A huge domestic argument had led to a physical altercation between my parents. My mom couldn't find her car keys, so she got us out of the house on foot.

We hid behind hedge rows and trees as we made our way toward the one home where my mom knew we'd be safe. It was the only place to find love, acceptance, and help in the middle of the adversity we were going through.

We were headed to Joyce's house. She was my mom's dearest friend. For many years, her family lived next door to us. Theirs was a friendship that would last a lifetime.

We had some great times together, taking unplanned road trips and visiting back and forth as if our houses were each an extension of the other. Love flowed, and there was much laughter.

A true friend loves you not just when you're standing on the peaceful mountaintop—but will also hold one hand while your other hand wields a sword in the battles of life fought in the deepest valleys. The roots of that type of friendship run deep. They triumph over the test of time. Life happens, and people move on, but those ties are a lifelong connection.

A few years ago, I took my mom on a trip to our hometown. She hadn't been there in decades. She hadn't seen Joyce for over forty years.

For as long as I breathe, I will not forget Joyce's look of surprise when she saw my mother's face. The embrace was ferocious as tears flowed. What a joyous reunion!

That was the last time they would ever see each other. The very next day, Joyce received her cancer diagnosis. She put up a tremendous fight, and the two of them kept in touch on social media. Even across the miles, my mother offered support and encouragement.

Through the hard relationships, the bad days, and the health battles, a true friend loves at all times. A friend like that is one to hang on to.

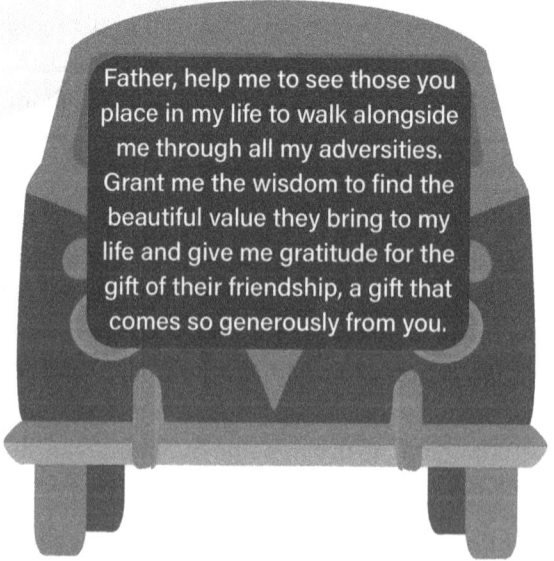

Father, help me to see those you place in my life to walk alongside me through all my adversities. Grant me the wisdom to find the beautiful value they bring to my life and give me gratitude for the gift of their friendship, a gift that comes so generously from you.

He "Hearts" Me

by Susan Stitch

May the Lord lead your hearts into a full understanding and expression of the love of God and the patient endurance that comes from Christ.

2 THESSALONIANS 3:5 (NLT)

IT WAS A really tough season. Within thirty days, two members of our household were diagnosed with cancer, another broke his elbow and needed surgery, and a fourth was diagnosed with whooping cough, causing our entire household to be quarantined. I was the only healthy one of the bunch, but with all the stress, I began experiencing heart palpitations. We had recently moved, and we didn't have a strong church connection yet, so it was easy to feel alone.

I knew God was in control, but with the numerous doctor visits, recuperating patients, and uncertain treatment plans, I was exhausted. I regularly cried out to God with tears running down my face, wondering why all this had to happen at once. I struggled not to worry. Did God even hear my prayers? I woke up each day wondering what disaster would befall us in the next twenty-four hours.

One morning, while making my instant flavored coffee, I dumped a spoonful of sweet, creamy powder into a cup of hot water. To my surprise, foamy bubbles rose to the top in the shape of a perfect heart.

I burst into tears. While this probably wasn't a message from God, it was definitely a reminder that he loved me and that he was in every aspect of our lives—even my coffee cup! Since then, I have randomly found hearts in nature when I need that reminder most. It might be a heart-shaped rock on a trail, a heart-shaped leaf that has fallen on my path, or even a heart-shaped cloud in the sky. I am careful to remind myself that this is not proof of his love because then if I didn't find one, I might think he didn't love me that day.

Instead, this is a gentle, natural reminder that the God of the universe created me and loves me no matter what I'm going through. He wants me to remember him and turn to him in every situation.

God, thank you for your incredible, personal love. Help me discover a tangible reminder of your love today. May I learn to love you with all my heart, all my soul, and all my might.

Love Silenced the Wolves

by Charlaine Martin

"A new commandment I give to you, that you love one another: just as I have loved you, you also are to love one another. By this all people will know that you are my disciples, if you have love for one another."

JOHN 13:34–35 (ESV)

QUIETLY, I BRACED myself for our accusers' final jabs at my pastor-husband—and me. But they said nothing. This wolf pack, who previously launched a vicious attack on us, filed silently past my husband's casket during the memorial service. It seemed as if God clamped their mouths shut. "Thank you, Lord. What a relief!" I sighed.

My heart went out to some congregation members who loved us and benefitted from our ministry. As their tears flowed while passing by me, I hugged them and prayed with them. Afterward, the funeral home director loaded Don's casket to transport his body to our hometown for his funeral.

Anger surged through me at how these power players had treated us. I couldn't grasp the depths of evil in controlling church leaders who maligned him, and me, while he battled terminal cancer. The pummeling took its toll on me in addition to all we endured with Don's cancer.

I decided to attend a spiritually healthy church in a nearby town. There, I could begin healing and forgive them. During a small group study on forgiveness, God prompted me to let go.

So, I prayed, "Lord, I forgive them. They don't grasp the damage they caused. I give them over to you to deal with their sin. It's not up to me. Thank you so much. In Jesus's name, amen." Freedom flooded my soul.

I look back now and can love them from a distance, not because of anything within me but because of the love of Christ. He not only forgave my sin but also theirs. Would I go back to that church? No. But I can pray for them and wish them well. Jesus's love silenced the voices of the wolves in my head and heart.

Jesus shared some last-minute instructions with his disciples before his arrest—his desire that they love each other as he had loved them. Those instructions stand true for us today. Indeed, anger is reasonable when we've been wronged, but holding grudges eats away at us and our relationships. Forgiveness is the first step toward freedom from the wolves in our lives. We know we have forgiven and moved on when we can pray for them and wish them well.

Lord God, I am hurt by what some people have done to me. I can't love them on my own. I give them and my pain to you. Help me love them as you have loved me.

Love That Keeps Us Together

by Joni Topper

"I have revealed you to them, and I will continue to do so. Then your love for me will be in them, and I will be in them."

JOHN 17:26 (NLT)

"TASTE THIS." MY husband cut off a piece of peach with his pocketknife. He reached my direction with the fresh fruit still resting on the blade, juice dripping. This was his way of loving me—sharing this piece of yummy goodness.

Another day, he said, "Come here. I want to show you something." He motioned me to follow him to the pasture. As I rounded the corner of the barn, two wobbly-legged baby goats appeared. For two weeks, we'd been watching for their entrance into this world. Now, here they were. Fresh. New. Perfect. The joy of seeing them for the first time was not complete until we shared it with each other.

My husband also knows that I watch for hummingbirds in the spring. For me, the sound of them buzzing around the feeders signals the changing season. Often, I have feeders out for a couple of weeks before the birds show up. "Did you hear that?" I'll call out to him when they arrive because he asks me every day if I've seen a hummer yet.

With each experience we share, we become *one* more and more. I think Jesus knew that shared experiences drew people closer. That may be why he wanted his disciples to know God—to know *him*. Perhaps the reason he longed to share God's love with them was because he knew once they experienced it, they would want to share it with others too.

I can tell you about someone I love all day long, and it will not impact you nearly as much as the time you spend with them forming your own relationship. Jesus could not wait for his disciples to know his Father as he did. The words of this verse were spoken in prayer. Jesus wanted his disciples to experience the same closeness with God that drove him to invite others into a relationship. His love for them was evident in the way he longed for them to be changed forever by that love. He did not want his disciples to miss one single good thing.

Jesus, thank you for sharing your love for the Father with me and through me. As I go about my day, help me exude your presence living in me so well that those I meet will want to know you better too.

God's Love Outshines Despair

by Natasha Lynn Daniels

Three things will last forever—faith, hope, and love—and the greatest of these is love.

1 CORINTHIANS 13:13 (NLT)

"BOGDANA GRACE, YOU are so pretty. You have beautiful eyes. Daddy will never let you get married," I teased her.

She shrugged and said, "I'm going to be like Rapunzel, except I don't have a mom that stole me from another mom!"

I looked at her and laughed, "Well, I kind of did!"

Bogdana Grace's face was priceless as she thought about it. She said, "Oh yeah! Forget what I just said, but at least it was legal, and I wanted to be with you!" We both laughed and hugged. I asked if she had forgotten, and she said, "Yes!"

My husband and I adopted Bogdana Grace from an orphanage in Ukraine. She had a rigid life of abuse and neglect. She endured things no little girl should ever have to experience at such a young age. The beauty through it all is that God had a plan for her life, and I am so thankful it included me becoming her mommy. She had sustained more difficulties in her life than simplicity, yet she forgot that she was adopted!

During that conversation, I was reminded of God's love. When we are full of his faith, hope, and love, and we follow him and cling to his joy, his love outshines the despair we once endured.

Faith is the premise and essence of God's message. It gets us through the complex seasons of our lives. Hope is the belief and anchor we cling to—it helps us know there is beauty in our ashes.

Jesus's love reminds us that we are precious to him, and he will never leave us. Love is the measure we give to ourselves, others, and the Lord. It is the greatest gift we have been given to remind us why we're here in the first place.

Bogdana forgot she was adopted because of the great love the Father bestowed on her through me, her daddy, friends, and family. She held fast to the good in her life, which is more potent than the tribulation she has faced.

When faith and hope are in order, we are unshackled to love fully because we understand how God loves us wholly.

Thank you, Lord, for the assurance of your love. It shines bright in my despair, filling me with faith, hope, and love when I accept it. Help me love others with the love you pour over me.

Nothing Shall Separate

by Susanne Moore

Who shall separate us from the love of Christ? Shall tribulation, distress, or persecution, or famine, or nakedness, or danger, or sword?

ROMANS 8:35 (ESV)

A LOT IS GOING on in the world today. So many hard things. Do you feel it in your soul? It's heartbreaking when there is no relief. As one problem ends, another begins. You might have trouble at your door right now. How can you know and trust God's love in the middle of your current struggle?

Take a glance at your personal history. Can you see how God's love remains steadfast? I can trace his love back to my childhood. My story tracks his rescue, provision, transforming grace, and overwhelming love for me. But it goes wider than our personal history. Examine world history, biblical history, and the history of Israel to see God's love and rescue of his people. If you have not done this, it's a deeply worthy journey to trust God's love for you.

The answer to the question, *Who shall separate us?* is powerful. Nothing and no one shall separate us from the love of Christ. That is substantial. It helps to circle back to how God showed his love for you during the hard times in your own life, especially when intrusive thoughts and doubts try to creep in. *Nothing*.

Not a friend or foe, not the Enemy, not a parent or a spouse or a child, and not even the world. God loved us so deeply that he promised to love us through it *all*. He sacrificed his Son for our eternal life, and he gave us the Holy Spirit to help us grapple with these doubts. Because of this, we can see his love in full motion for his glory.

> Heavenly Father, I bow before you to thank you for loving us beyond ourselves, our choices, and our sins. You made it known that you love me so dearly by sending Jesus to die on a cross so that I'm never separated from your love. I see your love at work now and through the battles yet to come. Keep me grounded in this hope.

The Choir Director's Miracle

by Beth Jennings Patch

For I am sure that neither death nor life, nor angels nor rulers, nor things present nor things to come, nor powers, nor height nor depth, nor anything else in all creation, will be able to separate us from the love of God in Christ Jesus our Lord.

Romans 8:38–39 (ESV)

OUR ADULT-SIZED CHOIR robes never motivated my older sister or me to act any more grown-up than we were as young teens. She signed random messages to me with her hands during the sermon, and I responded. We giggled quietly.

The choir director never said a word to us about it. We thought she couldn't hear or see us since she only faced us when we sang. Looking back on it, I believe Aunt Vinnie knew but allowed it because she wanted us in church, even if it meant overlooking our immature actions.

Decades later, this great-aunt and faithful servant of Jesus spent her days and nights out of touch with reality, lying in a single-size hospital bed, being spoon-fed by a stranger. I questioned in my heart why God would allow this saint to suffer in her later years on earth. My children and I visited her occasionally, and I tried to stay positive for everyone's sake. But it broke my heart to see her helpless and frail.

One stormy, cold afternoon, we stopped by to visit her.

Taking my aunt's hand, I said, "Oh my, it's good that you didn't have to go out in this cold storm."

She looked me in the eye and said, "Oh, but I did go out! Tommy and I went to Norfolk Wholesale Florist and the furniture store."

Her confident statement caught me by surprise. I knew she had been in her tiny bed all day, and Tommy had been with the Lord for over a decade. I paused and thought, *Why not go along with that? What she believes is so much better than what her actual day gave her.* I replied, "That's great. I'm so glad you two got to have a nice day together."

God revealed his truth to me in our brief visit. His love for Aunt Vinnie never abandoned her. Yes, reality escaped her, but God miraculously shielded her from the depressing knowledge of her physical and mental state. Instead, he lovingly filled this precious woman's mind with pleasant, loving times with her husband. I no longer questioned his love for our faith-filled aunt. Nothing in all creation can separate us from God's love.

> Father, your love knows no bounds. My narrow view of dismal events on earth often prevents me from seeing your love in action. Your thoughts are nothing like mine, and your ways are far beyond what I can imagine. Help me trust you and your inseparable love for me always.

The Gospel Is Love

by Pattie Reitz

Don't just pretend to love others. Really love them. Hate what is wrong. Hold tightly to what is good.

ROMANS 12:9 (NLT)

RECENTLY, I'VE SEEN several videos on social media that are similar in style and theme, and the focus is on the words being said with a tone that communicates a different meaning. A man looks at the camera and jokingly says, "Okay, guys, when your wife says she is *fine*, she is absolutely not fine! When you ask what is wrong and she says *nothing*, she does not mean nothing. Something is definitely wrong!"

While these videos are funny, they also touch on a timeless truth. Sometimes, a word being said does not communicate the message being sent. Instead, the tone tells the true story of what the person really means.

When I was young, I remember being told, "You are hearing, but you are not listening." As a person who deals with hearing loss, listening takes a conscious effort on my part. I also realize listening is vital for true communication. I catch myself hearing but not always listening, and realize I need to listen more carefully and lovingly to the meaning behind the words. Have you wrestled with this as well?

Whenever I consider love and words, I always come back to Jesus. The first chapter of the Gospel of John tells us, "So the Word became human and made his home among us."[a] Jesus *is* the Word of God! Later in the same Gospel, he told his disciples, "Love each other. Just as I have loved you, you should love each other."[b] Jesus also taught the Pharisees about love: "'You must love the LORD your God with all your heart, all your soul, and all your mind.' This is the first and greatest commandment. A second is equally important: 'Love your neighbor as yourself.'"[c]

When we fully listen to people, we can choose to respond with a loving spirit and communicate God's love as a balm to their pain or frustration. On the other side of the conversation, as we communicate to others, we can choose words that will tell the real story of what we are feeling so that we aren't tempted to say *fine* or *whatever*. This, too, shows love—the love of God for all people. In doing so, we share the gospel of Jesus.

Lord Jesus, when others share with me, more than anything, I want to listen to the message behind the words. Help me love them and respond with your love.

a John 1:14 (NLT)
b John 13:34 (NLT)
c Matthew 22:37–39 (NLT)

I Love You More

by Stacy Sanchez

Mercy, peace, and love be multiplied to you.

JUDE 1:2 (NKJV)

"I LOVE YOU ALL the way to the sky and around the moon, Mom-Mom." My grandson, Luca, and I like to play this game with one another. Who loves who more? We can devise some wacky examples of how big our love is as we each try to outdo the other.

"Well, I love you even more than that."

He smirked and retorted, "Oh yeah? I love you up to Jesus and back again."

"Hmmm, that's a lot. But I still love you even more."

"No, you don't, Mom-Mom! You can't love me more than up to Jesus. He loves us most of all."

"Good one. You're right, buddy. Jesus loves us most of all. You win."

Is there anything sweeter than a child's love for Jesus? Oh, that we were all as trusting as little children. When told how much Jesus loves them, they don't doubt it. They're all in. The more love, the better.

Why don't adults believe like children? What stops us from wholeheartedly accepting the extravagant love of Jesus as they do? Probably because we experience the pain of living in a broken world. We allow ourselves to become callous—even caustic—to an unseen Jesus who is supposed to love us. We doubt whether he can understand our world and what we go through. *Does he really love a person like me?*

As my grandchildren grow into adulthood and their faith matures, my prayer for them is this:

> May you hold on to the precious childlike love for Jesus and not become hardened by the pain and heartache of this world. May you come to a saving knowledge of Jesus, who loves you beyond anything words can describe—despite what you may have done. May you become mighty men and women of God who serve and honor him.
>
> May you experience the abundance of Christ's mercy—that you remember the compassion of our Lord, who covers our sins and failures and grants us undeserved forgiveness. More of his peace—that through the troubled times we all must walk, you feel the presence of the Holy Spirit, who carries you. And his love—that you overflow with the adoration of Jesus, drawing others to him.

My grandson was right; we cannot love more than "up to Jesus." He loves us most of all.

> Lord, Jesus, thank you for pouring out your abundance of mercy, peace, and love upon us. Father, help me accept this gracious gift and not become callous to your love. Open my heart to accept you even more.

No Regrets

by Joanie Shawhan

Love is patient and kind.

1 CORINTHIANS 13:4 (NLT)

"I'M STARVED! I haven't eaten all day." My friend scooted into her seat and grabbed the menu.

I exhaled, wishing one breath could release my pent-up tension. "I don't know about you, but I'm up for comfort food this evening. I can't believe we both moved our parents into assisted living on the same day. My life is summed up by the hashtag #LivingTheCrazy."

She laughed. "Our hashtag is #NoRegrets."

No regrets. As I deal with my aging mother in her varying stages of dementia, I want to live with no regrets.

The phone jingled. Mom. I sighed. The daily and sometimes multiple-times-a-day calls of "I don't feel good" had plucked my last nerve. A discordant outburst poised on the tip of my tongue. Mom was ninety-four. I couldn't fix ninety-four.

Her move was supposed to include new friends, fun activities, and communal dining. Instead, Mom skipped meals and retreated to her bed. She grieved the loss of her home, her independence, and her friends.

How could I help her? She vacillated between mild confusion, suspicion, and fragments of memory merging into a jumbled montage echoing past experiences. Somewhere buried beneath the dementia lay a person who needed love and respect.

Some days, I knew I made a difference. Seated on her patio, we laughed at pictures of her newest great-grandsons pulled up on my phone for the umpteenth time. Yet always new to her. We flipped through pages of books and identified the birds in the photographs.

On balmy days, we sat by the lake, listening to the waves and enjoying ice cream cones. Sometimes, we ventured out for a hamburger and strawberry shake, browsed for books, or drove through the countryside to admire the vibrant hues of autumn.

Mom loves music. I'd cajole her to get out of bed and go downstairs on live music days. She'd grumble and complain. But before long, her foot tapped and her head bobbed in time with the music. One of the entertainers in cowboy boots and hat invited her to dance. She beamed and extended her hand. Mom may not remember our phone calls and visits, but she remembers him.

God is teaching me that love is patient. And sometimes, he surprises me with joy.

My new hashtag? #NoRegrets.

Lord, when I'm feeling frustrated and overwhelmed in my role as caregiver, please fill my heart with your love. Help me to display your kindness and patience.

God's Appointment

by Joanie Shawhan

*Love never gives up, never loses faith, is always hopeful,
and endures through every circumstance.*

1 CORINTHIANS 13:7 (NLT)

NAOMI, HER HUSBAND, and two sons left their home in Israel during a famine and settled among people who worshipped pagan gods. Enter Ruth and Orpah, the Moabite women who married their sons. "Do not call me Naomi (sweetness); call me Mara (bitter), for the Almighty has caused me great grief and bitterness."[a]

Fast-forward ten years. Naomi's husband and two sons had died. She decided to return home. She had nothing to offer her daughters-in-law and insisted they return to their mothers' homes. But Ruth refused to comply. "Don't ask me to leave you and turn back. Wherever you go, I will go; wherever you live, I will live. Your people will be my people, and your God will be my God."[b]

Since they had no means of support, Ruth gathered grain the reapers left in the fields for the poor. But Ruth found favor with the wealthy landowner, Boaz, a relative of Naomi's husband.

Naomi hatched a plan. Boaz could buy the field belonging to Naomi's late husband, take Ruth as his wife, and raise an heir for her husband. Ruth followed her mother-in-law's instructions.

---

a   Ruth 1:20 (AMP)
b   Ruth 1:16 (NLT)

Naomi's plan worked. Ruth married Boaz and gave birth to a son, Obed, an ancestor of Jesus.

Naomi and Ruth each suffered a great loss, yet their reactions differed. Naomi despaired and lost hope. She allowed the bitterness of her situation to define her identity. Ruth endured similar circumstances, but her love for Naomi and belief in Naomi's God offered her hope for the future.

Even though their responses were different, God was faithful. In the end, he did exceedingly more than either Ruth *or* Naomi had ever dreamed possible. God is faithful, even when we are not.

Too often, I've responded to heartbreaks like Naomi. Bitterness chiseled away at my hope. I doubted God's faithfulness.

My desire is to endure life's challenges with the grace of Ruth—hope-filled and walking in love.

In my disappointment, may I discover God's appointment.

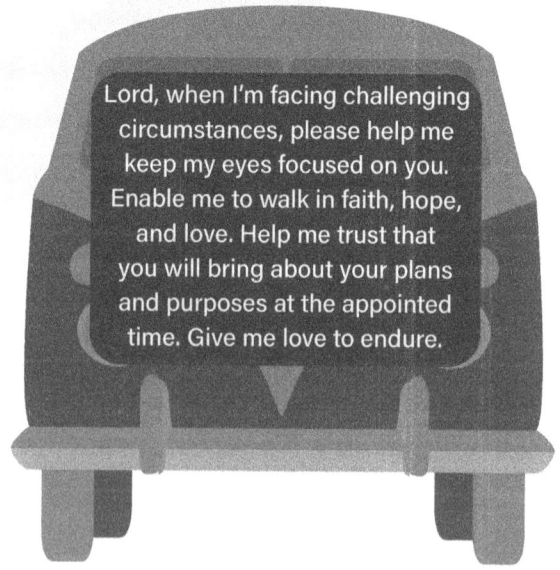

Lord, when I'm facing challenging circumstances, please help me keep my eyes focused on you. Enable me to walk in faith, hope, and love. Help me trust that you will bring about your plans and purposes at the appointed time. Give me love to endure.

Love Ain't So Crazy

by Hally J. Wells

Love never fails [it never fades nor ends]. But as for prophecies, they will pass away; as for tongues, they will cease; as for the gift of special knowledge, it will pass away.

1 CORINTHIANS 13:8 (AMP)

I SAT IN THE bleachers, singing and stomping to the latest fight songs. I wore my bright gold blazer and my bell-bottomed purple pants—both of the finest polyester—with a white blouse. This was the required, school-color-consistent pep club uniform. The songs were 1977 Queen hits, and they occupied the A and B sides of a 45 RPM single.

You know the ones. Classics now, they are still played in gymnasiums all around the country. Freddie Mercury declares a win and promises to *stone* the other team.

Mr. Mercury had another big hit. With a snappy beat and a relatable theme, he sang in 1979 about the bizarre and insane, small matter of love. That romantic love can be wacky, emotion-filled, and unreasonable. However, we can show God's love out in the world with complete sense, sanity, and reason.

Our church shows God's love with a simple thing each winter. We roll a clothing rack onto the sidewalk, and parishioners hang new or used coats for those without warm clothing or who are living unsheltered. The rack stays supplied and accessible throughout the cold months. I cherish hearing about other loving acts as well.

A female friend ministers to other women, helping them learn money-management skills, providing rides to work, and offering encouragement on dark days—all accompanied with prayer. Her life isn't perfect, but she makes room to help others. And even though my husband, who now drives a school bus, readily admits he's not a big fan of teens, he offered a bullied boy words of wisdom and kindness on one of his first days.

When we take a meal to a new mommy or praise the spread we enjoyed at a friend's home, we show kindness. When we offer our seat to an elderly person and patiently explain to a child why we did, we model care and compassion. When my nephew's public school basketball team prays together before their games and demonstrates good sportsmanship when they lose, they exhibit brotherly love.

What a difference love makes! Let's sing and stomp about that universal and timeless truth. Friends, loving gestures aren't little, and they surely aren't crazy. They aren't out of fashion like my color-clashing pep club getup. And if we look closely, they aren't as hard to find as the old 45s.

Heavenly Father, help me show love to those I encounter today. Please give me energy to extend a helping hand, gentle and wise words for any needing guidance, and compassionate hugs to those in despair.

Finding Comfort in the Chaos

by Beth Jennings Patch

For God has not given us a spirit of fear, but of power and of love and of a sound mind.

2 Timothy 1:7 (NKJV)

OH, HOW I wished I had some medical training. Dad had been alert all day—through the discharge from the hospital and the transport to this rehab facility. Now, he was taking a long nap.

"How long has he been sleeping?" the nurse asked me.

"A little over four hours."

"We need to run some tests, so we'll have to wake your father up," she said as she stood by his bed and called his name, "Doctor Jennings, we need you to wake up."

No response.

"Dr. Jennings? Dr. Jennings, we need you to wake up," she spoke louder.

No response.

She leaned in to hear Dad's breathing and touched his shoulder as she called out more. In seconds, three more medical people surrounded him. He was unresponsive.

Dad had suffered another heart attack. Soon, he was in an ambulance heading back to the hospital he had left early that morning. I couldn't believe this was happening! I was afraid he might die. Had I missed the signs he was in distress while he slept?

As I sat behind my steering wheel in the rehab parking lot, tears blurred my vision. *What am I doing here?* I asked myself. *I'm not the right person. I don't know anything about medical things.* I couldn't drive to the hospital, so I prayed. And in the quiet, cold night, I believe the Lord showed me his truth—I was there because of love. Because that's what love does—love shows up. Dad didn't need another medical person. He needed family. He needed me, and I was there.

This Bible verse embodied my experience, "God has not given us a spirit of fear, but of power and of love and of a sound mind."[a] God gave me the strength, love, and clear thinking to be with my dad on an extremely critical day. The enemy of my soul wanted me to fear that only someone with medical knowledge should be around my dad, and I wasn't her!

God's love won out. I visited Dad with confidence for the next several weeks of his life.

What fear has our enemy pestered you with? What is God's truth in your situation?

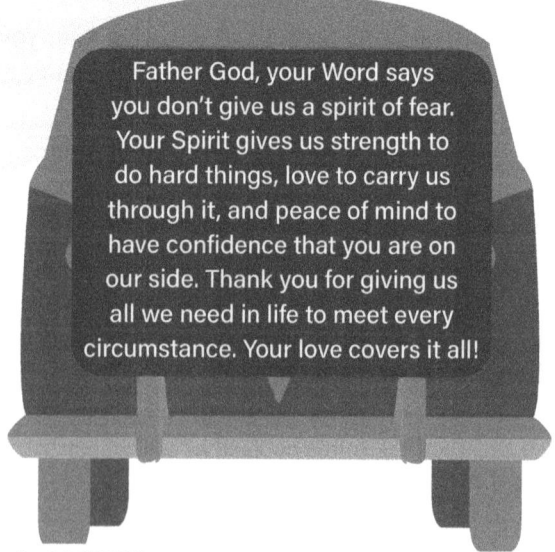

Father God, your Word says you don't give us a spirit of fear. Your Spirit gives us strength to do hard things, love to carry us through it, and peace of mind to have confidence that you are on our side. Thank you for giving us all we need in life to meet every circumstance. Your love covers it all!

---

a 2 Timothy 1:7 (NKJV)

From Fear to Comfort

by Missy Eversole

I love you, O Lord, my strength.

Psalm 18:1 (ESV)

TEARS FELL RAPIDLY down my face and onto the cement. Tired, weary, and stressed, the frustration over the lack of answers and progress made me tremble in anger.

Why aren't the doctors doing more?

Why didn't I push harder and insist we go to the hospital instead of waiting it out?

Why didn't God hear our prayers?

Our family was in a trial like we've never faced before. Our nineteen-year-old son had developed an extremely high fever and was hospitalized. Tests after test returned negative for all the common sicknesses, yet Connor's persistent fever continued to rise.

As a mom, I felt helpless. It's my job to protect my children, regardless of their age. Moreover, everything was out of my control, which drove me to desperation. I walked around the hospital block and found an empty metal bench.

Sitting down to gather my thoughts, I felt the heat from the bench burn my legs. The burning sensation was nothing compared to my hardened heart toward God. As I felt the hot July sun on my shoulders, a single tear fell from my eyes, and soon I was sobbing. While my mouth didn't speak the words, my heart did.

Where are you, God?

Immediately after crying out and asking God that question, I felt a peace I cannot adequately describe. I sensed God's presence. He was beside me on the hot bench, comforting me even as I questioned his whereabouts.

Although we still didn't have all the answers, God was with us all along. He was there when we walked into the ER, and a room was available. He was there when the doctors ran every test imaginable, stayed after hours, and would not rest until they found out what was causing the high fevers. He was there every second of our stay.

Two hours after my meltdown on the bench, the doctors informed us that Connor had pneumonia. We didn't realize it then, but our strength to get through those days was from God. He was our rock, and we saw his love through it all.

On those days when you feel the Lord has abandoned you, remember what David said after he was delivered from his enemies and Saul. "I love you, O Lord, my strength."[a] God is there. Lean on him for strength.

Father, on those days when I struggle, may I seek your presence over my circumstances. Please remind me that you are there and help me focus on you for comfort.

---

a   Psalm 18:1 (ESV)

The One Tree

by Lisa-Anne Wooldridge

That Christ may dwell in your hearts through faith; that you, being rooted and grounded in love, may be able to comprehend with all the saints what is the width and length and depth and height—to know the love of Christ which passes knowledge; that you may be filled with all the fullness of God.

EPHESIANS 3:17–19 (NKJV)

SUNLIGHT FLASHED THROUGH the trembling yellow aspen leaves, covering the forest floor in dancing pinpoints of light. Hundreds of slim white trunks, dotted with dalmatian spots, rose against an azure sky with crowns of gold. The forest stretched as far as I could see, and the beauty of it had me shouting glory. *What am I seeing here? I can barely take it in.* I whispered a little prayer of gratitude to the Artist, closing my eyes for a moment to impress the image into memory.

"That's all one tree, you know."

"How can that be? There are hundreds, no, thousands of trees there."

My husband was right. I learned that the trembling aspen forest was all one big living organism. Every trunk had grown up from the same root system, each one connected to all the others, sharing the same source and sustenance.

"I see men like trees."[a] The words of a blind man in the midst of being healed a couple thousand years ago came to mind.

---

a   Mark 8:24 (NKJV)

I imagined the aspen forest with people instead of trees—a body of believers standing shoulder to shoulder, arms linked, beautiful in their unity.

Sometimes, we don't know how big—how deep, how wide, how full—the love of God is because we have a limited vantage point. We might not be able to see the forest for the trees, as the saying goes. But it's only when we realize that we're rooted and grounded in love *with* all the saints that we start to understand the scope of God's love. His love passes understanding, but we can know it better in our union with him and each other.

We were designed to be filled with all the fullness of God and to comprehend his love, but believers can't do it alone. Like the aspen trees, we are all children of the same Father, living and moving and having our being in him.[a]

As we perceive that we are "the same tree" with our brothers and sisters, we get a clearer view of his love. We begin to see how massive and beautiful the forest is when we back up and get a God's eye view of the trees. When I look at you, I see me. I see us, and we are one in his love.

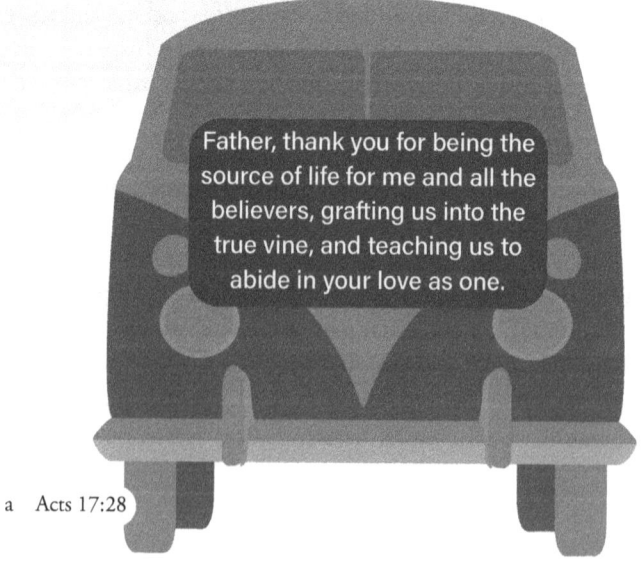

Father, thank you for being the source of life for me and all the believers, grafting us into the true vine, and teaching us to abide in your love as one.

a   Acts 17:28

That's Mine!

by Sally Ferguson

Speak the truth in love, growing in every way more and more like Christ, who is the head of his body, the church. He makes the whole body fit together perfectly. As each part does its own special work, it helps the other parts grow, so that the whole body is healthy and growing and full of love.

Ephesians 4:15–16 (NLT)

"THAT'S *MY* KETCHUP!"

Four pairs of eyes locked on me in shock at my outburst. We had just come through a harrowing ordeal on a busy highway when my tire popped, and a piece of flashing flew from the side of the car. After navigating safely to the berm and catching a ride in a massive tow truck, we were now tucked in for a bite to eat while waiting for new tires at the shop. Happy, almost delirious, that we lived to tell about our accident.

Now I decided to have a meltdown? *Over ketchup?* Shock turned into merriment as laughter ensued. My friends realized stress had caught up with me and gave me hugs—and more ketchup.

That wild ride from our writers' getaway became a legendary part of our adventure as friends. We posed for pictures with the tow truck and repeated the story of our survival. We laughed at condiments and poked each other again for fun. I found an anonymous meme that represents us—gal friends bent over laughing,

"Blessed are we, who can laugh at ourselves. For we will never cease to be amused."

I could have felt as if the others were laughing *at* me, but there was something added to the moment. Love was the distinction. I knew they were in the thick of things *with* me, and that made all the difference. That's my circle of friends who love me.

Life never ceases to provide opportunities to laugh at myself as I react and respond to the world. I'm thankful for the love from friends and family as we travel this globe, even if it means sharing my ketchup.

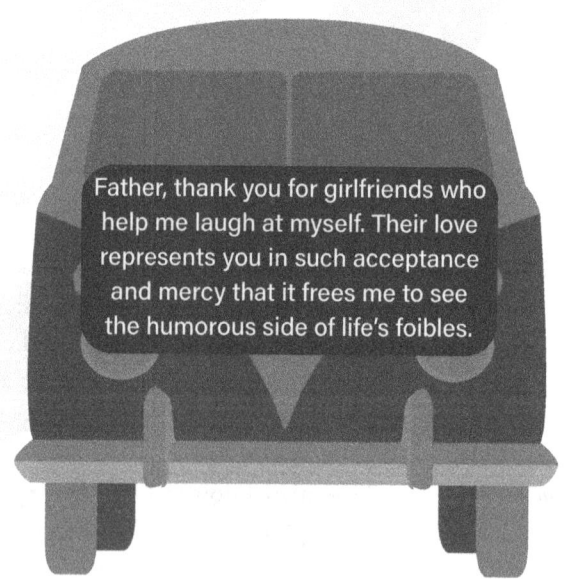

Father, thank you for girlfriends who help me laugh at myself. Their love represents you in such acceptance and mercy that it frees me to see the humorous side of life's foibles.

This Moment Is Proof

by Robin Steinweg

And walk continually in love [that is, value one another—practice empathy and compassion, unselfishly seeking the best for others], just as Christ also loved you and gave Himself up for us, an offering and sacrifice to God [slain for you, so that it became] a sweet fragrance.

EPHESIANS 5:2 (AMP)

HOW WAS I talked into this? Teeth clenched, I followed my ecstatic young son onto the ski lift. The narrow slats of ash and foam attached to my boots touched nothing but frosty air. I death-gripped whatever there was of that flimsy, open seat to grip. My stomach lurched. Or it might have been the ski lift moving. Or the ground falling away below.

I felt sick.

My son's excitement penetrated the terror, and I spoke, my words hanging quietly in the cold like icicles. "If you ever—*ever*—doubt that I love you, remember this moment. *This* moment is proof that I love you."

He grinned and patted my glove. Nothing broke when I fell off the ski lift trying to disembark, and I didn't disgrace the family name by begging to be driven back down the slope instead of balancing on two skinny sticks. I may never slalom, but at least my son knows I love him!

Jesus loves us more.

I joke about sacrificing myself on the slopes because I value my son and want the best for him. What else does a caring parent do?

But what really takes the breath away is the astounding fact of Jesus's love for us. The perfect and holy Son of God, the creator of all that exists, loves us. Loves us to the point of becoming a physically frail human being and allowing himself to be killed as the perfect sacrifice to pay for our sin—*my* sin—with his blood, his life. Such love!

His love transforms us into beings capable of his kind of love. He enables us to be compassionate and unselfish, wanting the best for others. Practicing empathy. And yes, sometimes it takes practice!

So, if you or I ever—*ever*—doubt that God loves us, remember the moment Jesus died on the cross. *This* moment is proof that he loves us.

God of love, there is no greater love than what Jesus showed for us, dying on the cross. Thank you that if I ever doubt your love, I can point to that moment as absolute proof. Help me to love like you.

Love the Name

by Sandy Lipsky

"O LORD, God of my master, Abraham," he prayed. "Please give me success today, and show unfailing love to my master, Abraham."

GENESIS 24:12 (NLT)

WHEN I WAS born, my mother wanted to name me Donneiletta—a combination of her name, DorEtta, and Dad's name, Neil. Mom loved her own unique name, and she wanted me to love my name too.

Although Dad insisted my name be Sandra, Mom's infectious appreciation for names rubbed off on me. And when I became a Christ follower, the meaning of names took on a greater significance. Especially when my husband and I found out we would be parents.

I became obsessed with choosing the perfect name for our adopted baby. My husband and I agreed easily on a boy's name but not a girl's. When we received the call that our baby girl had been born, we had to figure out what we would call her. Excited but panicked, I begged the Lord for guidance. *We only have the length of this car ride to find the perfect name, Father. Please help.*

While Jon drove, I read off girl names from my baby book. "Let's start with the A's." My husband responded with an immediate, "Good idea."

The process took about thirty seconds. When I said, "Alexandra," I saw him nod.

"Alexandra is a variation of Sandra," I said.

"How about Alexandra Michelle?" my husband asked. "Then she'll be named after both of us. Her first name after you and her middle name after my middle name since Michelle is the feminine form of Michael."

Once we arrived at the hospital, we met our daughter and then her birth mother, Beth.* As we chatted in the hospital room, she inquired what we would call our baby. She seemed pleased with our choice.

The next day on the obstetrics floor, our daughter's birth great-grandmother was rocking her in a room adjacent to the nursery. After sharing pleasantries, she asked, "Who chose the name?"

"We did," I responded.

"I don't know if you realize that Beth wrote poetry in high school. She used the pen name Alex to sign her work."

Chill bumps formed. I had recently asked God to affirm our name selection. What wonderful confirmation. The Lord's unfailing love never ceases to surprise me.

*Name changed.

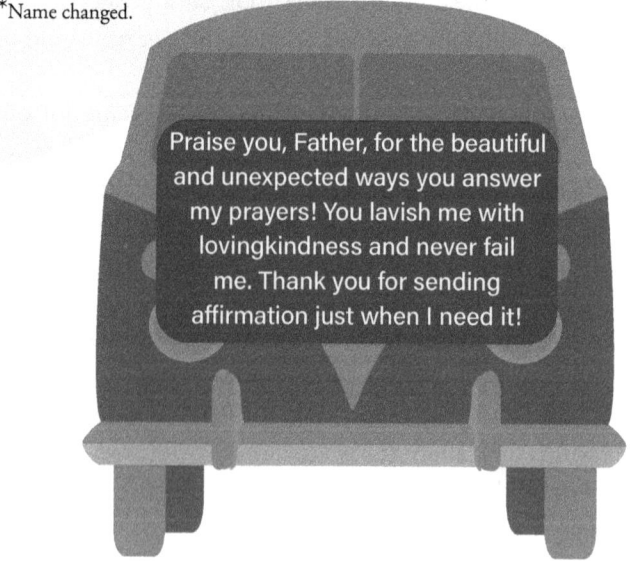

Praise you, Father, for the beautiful and unexpected ways you answer my prayers! You lavish me with lovingkindness and never fail me. Thank you for sending affirmation just when I need it!

Viv's Mission of Love

by Denise Margaret Ackerman

And let us consider [thoughtfully] how we may encourage one another to love and to do good deeds.

HEBREWS 10:24 (AMP)

MY ARMS WERE too short, and I needed more than two hands to keep my active toddlers under control. The long wooden church pew might as well have been a football field when it came to containing my wild ones by myself! Our small country church didn't provide nursery care during the Sunday evening service. Although I knew it would be challenging to keep three-year-old Michelle and two-year-old twins Michael and Matthew quietly occupied during the hour-long service, I *had* to attend. I was a young Christian who yearned to learn from God's Word and fellowship with other believers.

The evening service had just begun when Mike, brown eyes gleaming with mischief, jogged left while Matt swiftly dove under the pew in front of us. Before I could decide which one to tackle, Vivian came from behind us and smoothly slid into place at the end of our pew to block Mike's way of escape. A seasoned pro at handling toddlers, Auntie Viv pulled out pencils and paper and invited Mike to trace the outline of his hand. Matt, not wanting to miss out on his brother's new pastime, turned back from his adventure and climbed up next to them.

Viv's mission of love was successful! With both boys entertained and Michelle nestled beside me, I breathed a sigh of relief as I opened my Bible to refocus my frazzled thoughts on Pastor's message.

We spent future Sunday evening services seated together with Auntie Viv. Always equipped to bless me and my little ones, Viv's selfless acts of love taught me how the Lord desires his followers to care for each other.

As our congregation grew, the church eventually added nursery care for evening services. Even though my role as a mom was challenging, I volunteered to be on the schedule. This was my opportunity to help other young moms receive the same blessing Viv had given me.

Our dear church family blessed and encouraged us many times over the years. When my husband injured his back, men came to split firewood. During a difficult financial season, we received donated groceries. Church members provided childcare during my hospitalization.

The countless loving deeds showered on my family set an example for me to follow—teaching me to be on the lookout for ways to express God's love to those in need of encouragement.

Dear Father, thank you for the many believers who have helped and encouraged me in my Christian walk. Please help me to notice those who need a loving act of encouragement and find meaningful ways to share your love with them.

Hope for Tomorrow

by Joanie Shawhan

The steadfast love of the LORD never ceases; his mercies never come to an end; they are new every morning; great is your faithfulness.

LAMENTATIONS 3:22–23 (ESV)

FIRESTORMS—THOSE UNEXPECTED, devastating losses that disrupt our lives. I have experienced several firestorms in my life: the loss of loved ones, an ovarian cancer diagnosis, and shattered dreams. Sorrow and grief singed me. I wondered if I would survive. But God's love is faithful.

The prophet Jeremiah also experienced firestorms. For forty years, Jeremiah warned his fellow countrymen that God's judgment would come if they did not turn back to God. He was rejected by family and friends, imprisoned, thrown in a dungeon, and suffered starvation. He pleaded with kings to no avail and lost his homeland to an invading army. Left homeless, he was carried away to Egypt in captivity.

Jeremiah wept as he penned his lament in the book of Lamentations, his heart broken over the devastation of his homeland. Suddenly, his tone changed. He praised the love and faithfulness of God. He found hope in God's mercies. What happened to Jeremiah's lament? He still mourned over the state of his homeland. But he realized God was bigger than his pain and suffering.

Amid his grief, Jeremiah hoped. A hope he offers us today.

I also have experienced God's love and faithfulness amid firestorms. But as we see with Jeremiah, surviving a firestorm doesn't imply everything is all better. True triumph is not necessarily a return to life before the firestorm, but it is a heart attitude—is God still God despite my pain and loss? I believe Jeremiah discovered that God was still God. The God who never changes.

Along with Jeremiah, I can proclaim that God is still God. His love never fails. In our brokenness, God promises us a tomorrow.

Lord, please help me remember when I am hurting that you are faithful and your love for me never changes. May I always anticipate my tomorrows, filled with your compassion and mercy.

Safe in God's Love

by Pattie Reitz

But you, dear friends, must build each other up in your most holy faith, pray in the power of the Holy Spirit, and await the mercy of our Lord Jesus Christ, who will bring you eternal life. In this way, you will keep yourselves safe in God's love.

JUDE 1:20–21 (NLT)

COMPARISON HAS THE potential to steal our joy. As people living in the twenty-first century, we inhale information from all sides, from social media loaded down with quips and memes to everyone posting photos of vacations and humblebrags of accomplishments. It's a lot to take in, and it's easy to fall into the trap of comparing our less-than-perfect reality with everyone else's picture-perfect posts. In the middle of it all, sometimes our faith in God can feel far away.

How can we, as modern-day Christians, help each other grow and unite in faith? How can we tune in to God's still small voice among all the noise in our world? How can we avoid tempting comparison traps? Jude tells those who are called by God to build each other up and pray for each other. Sounds great, but what does that look like today?

One way we can show love is with encouragement. During times I've felt like a failure, the Lord encouraged me through loving words from a friend. At other times, the Holy Spirit helps me encourage friends right where they are—with their children, with their work, in their spiritual walk. The apostle Paul wrote, "So encourage each other and build each other up, just as you are already doing."[a] We can apply this verse to ourselves as well. How? By not tearing ourselves down through comparisons with others, in person or online.

The apostle Jude encouraged believers to pray in the Spirit. In contrast, when we talk to God in our own strength and only for our own needs and wants, we are not building our faith. However, if we focus on the Holy Spirit, who helps us pray even when we don't have the words ourselves,[b] we commune with God on a much deeper level. This connection with Christ is good for our hearts and our faith.

As we seek to know our Savior more intimately, let's ask for opportunities to show love to the people God places in our lives with encouragement and prayer. These two practices help drown out the shouts of comparison that are so prevalent in our world while also working to strengthen our relationships with each other and with our loving God.

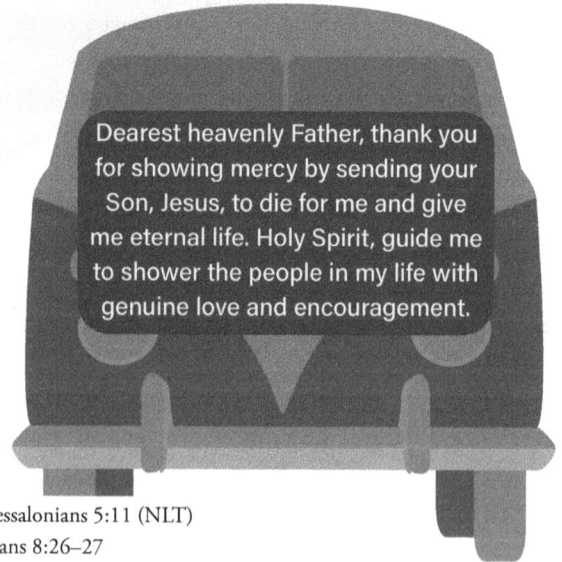

Dearest heavenly Father, thank you for showing mercy by sending your Son, Jesus, to die for me and give me eternal life. Holy Spirit, guide me to shower the people in my life with genuine love and encouragement.

a   1 Thessalonians 5:11 (NLT)
b   Romans 8:26–27

The God Who Bends Down

by Becki James

I love the LORD because he hears my voice and my prayer for mercy. Because he bends down to listen, I will pray as long as I have breath!

PSALM 116:1–2 (NLT)

"DADDY! DADDY!" THE little girl sobbed, feeling alone and afraid as she ran across the playground. Tears wet her face, causing thin blonde strands to stick to her dirt-smudged cheeks. Her tiny limbs stumbled over the bumpy mulch. *Thud!* With a face full of pine bark, she looked up to see her father.

The man took a few strides, knelt down, and gently brushed the hair out of her eyes and the dirt from her skin. Sitting beside her, he opened his arms, motioning for her to climb into his embrace.

The little girl scooted to her knees and crawled onto his lap. Pressing her head safely against his chest, she whispered, "Oh, Daddy, I'm so glad you heard me."

※❀※❀※❀※

Why do I love the Lord? Simple. He hears me. How do I know he hears me? Because he answers my prayers.

Prayer is an extraordinary gift. At any time or place on the planet, the God who created the universe listens to us. No prayer is too long or too short. No voice is too loud or too soft. He hears and answers them all.

Maintaining childlike faith in our heavenly Father requires spiritual maturity. We need to be wise enough to keep an uncomplicated trust in him. Consider a toddler who barely understands language yet instinctively seeks parental refuge. Developing this kind of confidence in God requires us to put aside our grown-up self-reliance. We adults mask our fears and faults to appear poised and perfect. I am in my fifth decade of life, yet I sometimes act like an immature brat. I fall down, point fingers, throw fits, and am terribly impatient. (*Ouch!*) In contrast to that behavior, having childlike faith adopts a kid's ability to exude transparency in their trust.

I love the Aramaic word for father—*abba*. When Jesus prayed, he called Father God by this intimate name.[a] Believers in Christ's redemptive work on the cross are adopted into the privilege of calling on Father through his Holy Spirit within us.[b] When I read Psalm 116, I envision it is Abba who bends down to listen to me. He hears my cry for mercy, brushes the dirt of my sin out of my eyes so that I can see his face again, and welcomes me into his arms.

Abba, Father, I am grounded in your love for me. Thank you for bending down to hear me and for answering my prayers. I love you, Lord, and I will lift my voice to you as long as I have breath!

a Mark 14:36
b Romans 8:15

Borrowed Fruit

by Sandy Lipsky

But the Holy Spirit produces this kind of fruit in our lives: love, joy, peace, patience, kindness, goodness, faithfulness, gentleness, and self-control. There is no law against these things!

Galatians 5:22–23 (NLT)

I NEVER KNEW THE young man, but his life impacted mine. He collapsed at work and died suddenly one day, leaving behind a wife and two young children. Hundreds gathered at his funeral held at a large, local church. His wife, who, years prior, had been a student at the school where I taught, shared a powerful testimony of his life. What impressed me as I watched the service on YouTube was how a man so young exhibited the fruit of the Spirit with so much finesse.

The description of his love for others produced a stirring in my own heart. It's hard to articulate what happened as I listened to the eulogy. It felt as if a baton passed from him to me in relation to a particular story his wife told.

He began a ministry for widows while in his twenties. This youthful man of God began a yearly act of kindness. On Valentine's Day, he would deliver a single red rose to the women in his church who had lost a spouse. The busyness of life did not keep him from this quiet and faithful deed.

I can only imagine how valued each widow felt as this tall, handsome man approached her with a beautiful bloom. Did he remind them with this loving gesture that she was not alone or invisible? Could a seemingly small gesture display God's unfailing love?

A thought germinated as I continued to watch the ceremony online. *Both of our neighbors are widows, and at least four more live in the subdivision where I walk. Could I bring them flowers?*

The evidence of the Spirit I witnessed in this young man began to produce a longing in my own life to replicate his behavior. And for the past five years, I've delivered flowers and a note to my widowed neighbors. If I could, I would tell this brother in Christ that although many would say his life was cut short, he made an eternal difference here on earth.

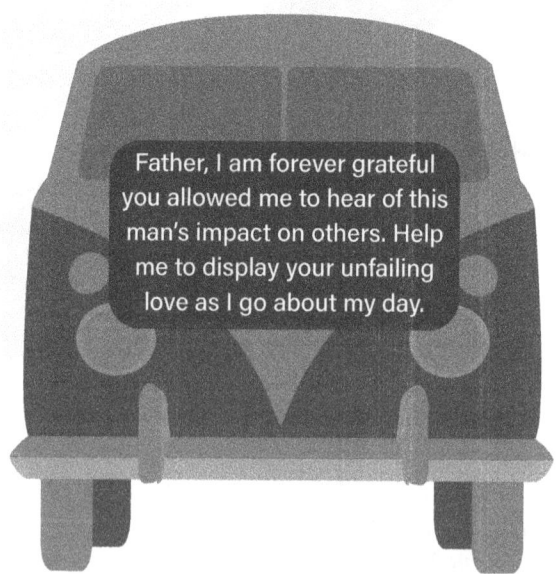

Father, I am forever grateful you allowed me to hear of this man's impact on others. Help me to display your unfailing love as I go about my day.

Lessons from the Fall

by Janice Metot

But let us who live in the light be clearheaded, protected by the armor of faith and love, and wearing as our helmet the confidence of our salvation.

1 THESSALONIANS 5:8 (NLT)

ONE MINUTE, I was on a mission; the next minute, I was on the floor. A burst of white light caused time to pause. I lay there stunned until the pounding in my head subsided, and my senses returned.

I was acutely sensitive to light, sound, and chaos for the next few months. Dizziness played in the background continually, affecting my concentration and draining me of vitality and energy.

During my recovery, I realized that I was struggling similarly as a Christian. I was easily distracted by conflicting messages blasting out like machine gun fire through the media. Overwhelmed by my encounters with people, I often felt attacked, wounded, and defeated. I had no peace. Just as it would never occur to me to wear a helmet for protection, I did not realize my mindset left me vulnerable to influences that eroded at my heart and motivation.

Spiritual armor is not easily understood. The juxtaposition between wearing a tangible helmet with armor when compared to the ideas of salvation, faith, and love is striking. The former sets a scene of heavily clad soldiers fighting violent battles. The latter produces images like Jesus on the cross, someone kneeling in prayer, and a mother cradling her child. Protective gear is temporal, defensive, and cumbersome—while the armor of God is eternal and offensive, allowing freedom in movement.

Love is a double-edged sword in the context of salvation and faith, both our defense and our weapon. God's love poured out through Jesus Christ created a bridge crossing the divide between the cares of this world and his presence. Salvation brings us there. In faith, we travel back and forth freely, with the assurance of receiving the help we need. Love is the substance of salvation, the beginning and the end, sealing our identity as a child of God.

As Christians, our mission to live differently in the world is more difficult than ever. Love is the secret weapon that sets us apart. When we enter the presence of God's love, our resistance dissolves. There, we let go of the anger and fear clouding our judgment. Strengthened, we rise to respond rather than react because love does not fail. Putting on this imperishable armor brings the heart and mind into harmony, keeps us focused, and fuels our journey with meaning.

> Heavenly Father, thank you for your unsurpassed love that protects and keeps me. I ask for the clarity of mind to seek your presence quickly so that I do not try to handle things on my own. Help my unbelief when fear tries to take hold. Today, may I walk with great focus, mindful that your love has provided everything I need to overcome.

Secure in Love

by Becki James

"For the mountains may depart and the hills be removed, but my steadfast love shall not depart from you, and my covenant of peace shall not be removed," says the LORD, who has compassion on you.

ISAIAH 54:10 (ESV)

ELEVATION: 6,983 FEET. I walked out onto a platform on the top of Mt. Pilatus, Switzerland. A great hush nearly offset my footing. The stillness seemed alive—majestic and breathing. It settled onto me as if I'd entered a grand cathedral. Drawn to a stone wall overlooking the panorama, I peered over and beheld the vast congregation of earth below.

Astounding. Massive lakes reduced to the sprinkles of baptistry waters. Clouds strewn out like linen hanging on air and draping shadows on the hills below. I blinked at the immensity, turning my head to capture the entire scope. It was real. I marveled to share in this expanse. I felt small. Very small. *God—this is what you see? How am I so fortunate to catch this tiniest glimpse of your mighty perspective?*

The wind rippled over distant peaks, lifting my hair across my cheeks. It filled the summit with a voice that echoed deep down into the valley. I closed my eyes to listen. The sound drifted as an angelic chorus ringing praises to their Creator. Snowcapped spires towered on every side. The sky stretched upward into the heavens. This massive rock that held me so high was a mere footstool in God's infinite sanctuary. And yet, I stood tall. God's presence embraced me with the power of his love.

Long before I decided to trek up Mt. Pilatus, it stood strong and immovable. Withstanding the ages, it buffered weather patterns and served as a fortress in times of war and a hiding place for royalty. As I flew away from Switzerland to Italy, the Alpine range enamored me with awe. Hard to believe I was a dot atop just one of those massive tips. The idea of removing a whole mountain, let alone putting a dent in one, was inconceivable.

God says in Isaiah that even if the mountains cease to exist, his commitment of love remains secure. His love is eternal, enduring beyond this world I call home. Mountains are solid. They do not waver in the wind. But the most permanent landform diminishes to dust compared to the Lord's divine devotion. He is loyal. He is faithful. His compassion exceeds my comprehension. And within my Lord's steadfast love, I am safe, I am sheltered, and I am secure.

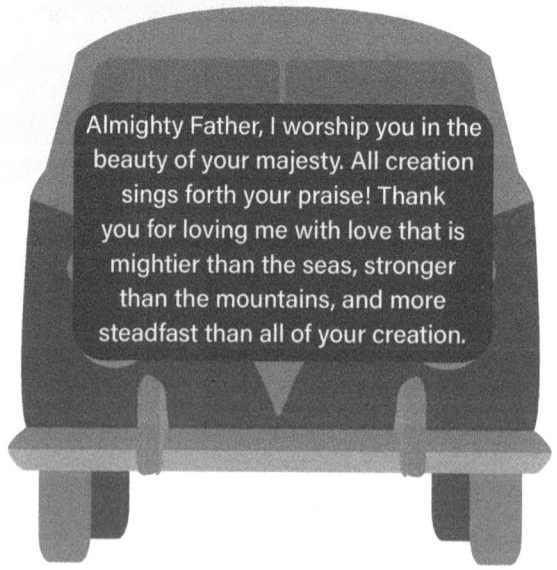

Almighty Father, I worship you in the beauty of your majesty. All creation sings forth your praise! Thank you for loving me with love that is mightier than the seas, stronger than the mountains, and more steadfast than all of your creation.

Joy

All Kinds of Joy

by Robin Steinweg

You will live in joy and peace. The mountains and hills will burst into song, and the trees of the field will clap their hands!

ISAIAH 55:12 (NLT)

I HAVE A CHRISTMAS figurine I keep in view all year. Every time I see it, I find myself grinning, and my heart swells. It's white like alabaster. Mary holds baby Jesus high, and they appear to have been twirling, by the motion of her skirts. As if they've been laughing together. It is titled "The Cause of Our Joy."

Memory bytes remind me of similar feelings.

Our firstborn son sat in a shopping cart steered by my mom at the back of a five-and-dime store, where they sold goldfish and canaries. I was a few aisles away, but his little voice sailed through the space: "The birdies! They're singing pwaise to God!" And then he started to sing the melody of Beethoven's "Ode to Joy" but in his toddler rendition: "Alleluia, Alleluia, Alleluia, pwaise da Lord!"

You know his mama's heart warmed, but it was way more than that. Joy welled up until I wanted to dance and sing praise to God myself for his awesomeness.

In a different sort of joyful moment, our second-born son sat in a highchair at our family's favorite diner.

"The waitress will bring your food in a minute," we told him. Moments later he suspiciously eyed the food the waitress set before him. His mind having been filled earlier with stories of castle strongholds, and with no understanding of what our server was called, he said, "What did the fortress bring, anyway?"

Laughter makes for good digestion!

Our sons grew, and the younger had a child. One December, our eldest was sick and missed Christmas, and our granddaughter was "so 'pointed." But when the door opened a week later to reveal him there, she squealed, "Uncle Daviiiiiiiid!" and blurred past us, jumping to throw herself at him. Unbridled exuberance.

Whether these moments seem faith-filled or not, they're still from God. He gifts us with joy.

Joy can find expression in leaping, shouting, singing, laughing, playing music, and dancing. Joy can be found in hard times—a more solemn version—a bedrock of wellbeing despite trials. It is an action and a choice. A pathway God gives to help us feel better. When we open ourselves to the fullness of his presence, joy fills us and spills over.

Even nature bursts with song. Listen! Are the hills singing? Are the trees clapping?

What kind of joy might we discover next?

You are the God who makes us smile. You turned water into fine wine at a wedding reception. You allowed Balaam's donkey to speak to him. You gathered up children to bless them. Remind me daily to embrace and share in your joy and laughter. There is joy in your presence!

How Do I Get That Joy?

by Joni Topper

> *"These things I have spoken to you, that my joy may be in you, and that your joy may be full."*
>
> JOHN 15:11 (ESV)

STAY FULL OF joy? Just how could Jesus give me *his* joy?

My friend Karen lived across the street when I was a little girl. We were more like sisters than friends. Our moms treated us as if we were siblings too. Karen's mom, Betty, instructed me when watching movies with her family, "Joni, you are welcome to stay but *not* to talk all the way through the movie."

If I kept talking, I'd miss the plot and then not understand the story, start asking questions, and interrupt everyone's experience.

Jesus instructed his disciples to listen too. Probably for the same reasons. He didn't want them to miss the main idea. "These things" that Jesus spoke of offered a recipe for joy, a map to find not basic joy but *full* joy. What he offered went beyond their own capacity to conjure up.

Jesus stressed to his disciples that if they abided in him—stayed close to him and let his words live in them—the result would be that they obeyed God and loved each other. He promised this would bring joy.

Those supernatural words of instruction, "Abide in me,"[a] summed up the formula to joy. To abide is to continue. Jesus wants us stay close to him and to look forward to the joy he gives.

---

a   John 15:4 (ESV)

Betty told me to stop talking and listen so that I'd understand. Jesus told his disciples to heed his words. Apart from him, Jesus pointed out, we would not be able to do anything for God.[a] Jesus's message—obey God's commandments, abide in his love, and be full of joy—sounds simple.

My neighbor Betty understood that unless I stayed engaged, I'd get confused about the movie. Jesus knows that if we don't stay engaged with his words, we'll get mixed up too.

People tend to want joy so much that they search for it. Jesus offered a "find joy" plan. Obey God's commandments, abide in his love, and you will have joy.

Lord, help me to abide in you so that I'll want to obey your commandments. Open my eyes so I will recognize your faithfulness in using my obedience to further your kingdom. Thank you for giving me joy in serving.

---

a John 15:5

A Two-Dollar Bill and Ice Cream

by Charlaine Martin

Complete my joy by being of the same mind, having the same love, being in full accord and of one mind. Do nothing from selfish ambition or conceit, but in humility count others more significant than yourselves. Let each of you look not only to his own interests, but also to the interests of others.

PHILIPPIANS 2:2–4 (ESV)

How dare he disrupt *the kids' school!* I fumed. "This is our kids' school time. We can't homeschool willy-nilly. Don't you have homework too?" I said.

"I wanted to watch morning cartoons with the kids," he replied, visibly annoyed.

My husband didn't understand my challenges in getting the kids to do their assignments. God had called him to be a pastor, so he began seminary, which meant studying at home. It was so new for us.

"What's this?" I asked. Frustrated, I surveyed the piles around his chair in view of the front door. *This will be a long three years for his MDiv degree.*

"I'll set up in the family room," he grumbled.

"No! That's our school space." Battle-weary, I insisted, "We need help finding a solution." He agreed. I needed designated school time and space for the kids' success, while Don needed to feel included in family life.

We met with our pastor, who welcomed us into his office. He listened without giving us answers. Instead, he pulled a two-dollar bill from his desk and handed it to Don. "You two get some ice cream together. Remember, use your polite words with each other."

That's it?

So, we went on our ice cream date. It had been a while, and it felt good. We began respecting each other with *please* and *thank you*. Slowly, our tug-of-war ceased. Don felt he belonged at home, and I could maintain a healthy homeschool environment for our kids.

Later, when our pastor visited us in our first church, his face lit up! He saw his two-dollar investment lived through our family. Even with inflation, our pastor's investment continues to multiply.

The Philippian church also had differing views that caused tension, so Paul encouraged them to set aside their agendas to unite in Christian love. Common faith joined them as one, becoming selfless and humble. Paul rejoiced in this congregation he loved so much. They became an example to all who watched them work, live, and worship together. Paul saw his teaching lived out in this congregation.

We can't embrace each other until we let go of the rope in our tug-of-war. Let's set aside our differences to unite Christ's love, looking to each other's interests. May people see our love lived out in our shared faith every day. Let's make Paul's—and our pastor's—joy complete. Go! Multiply that two-dollar investment on a date, fully loving each other.

Lord, I'm sorry when my selfish agenda divides my relationships. Please help us work together in Christian love and bring us peace.

I Will Joy

by Robin Steinweg

Though the fig tree may not blossom, Nor fruit be on the vines; Though the labor of the olive may fail, And the fields yield no food; Though the flock may be cut off from the fold, and there be no herd in the stalls—Yet I will rejoice in the LORD, I will joy in the God of my salvation.

HABAKKUK 3:17–18 (NKJV)

I WILL JOY. THAT'S a verb! How unusual to use it as an action word. Almost like saying we'll "Google" something. *I will joy.* It's a choice we make, an act of our will. There was a time I didn't know that option.

When I was a young teen, my best friend developed anorexia. I retreated inside myself, unable to understand or cope. I went through the motions of my days, unaware of lessons or assignments until a teacher knelt by my desk.

"I'm so sorry, Robin. You're getting a failing grade this quarter. How can I help?"

I hadn't turned in any work for a couple of months. Tears welled. The school contacted my parents with similar news about other classes. Everyone was kind. My folks came alongside to help me get back on track and end the semester with high grades. My friend was hospitalized and eventually recovered.

Following my freshman year of college, I thought I'd outgrown the problem until my closest aunt developed cancer and died. There I went, my mind blank for hours at a time. I accepted that this was how I handled hard things.

After college, while we were still in our early twenties, a friend shared with me about having faith in Jesus Christ. As I received God's gift of forgiveness and his indwelling Holy Spirit, he transformed me. I immersed myself in his Word.

A few months later when my mother-in-law died unexpectedly, I waited to disappear inside myself again. Instead, though the emotional pain was intense, something buoyed me up. A sense of absolute wellbeing ran beneath me. A firm footing held the weight of grief and didn't let me sink into oblivion.

What is this? I questioned myself, but the answer that instantly came to mind wasn't mine and surprised me. *This is joy.*

I had chosen to open my life to Jesus. He came in to stay. His presence filled me with joy. He and his joy have never left.

Because Jesus is here, no matter the loss, illness, or daily uncertainty, I can—and will—joy in my God!

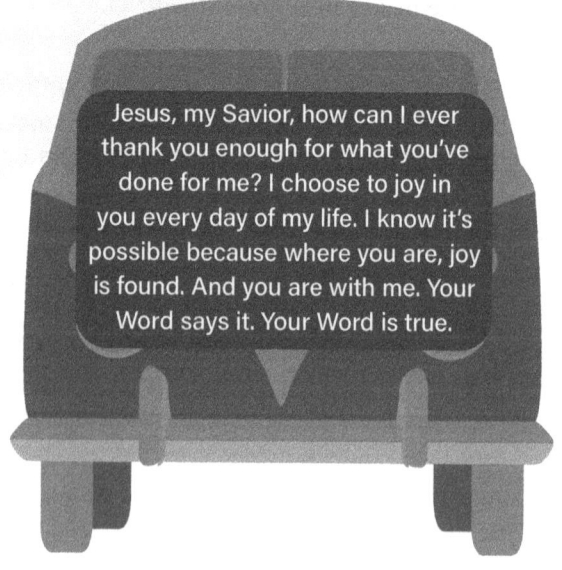

Jesus, my Savior, how can I ever thank you enough for what you've done for me? I choose to joy in you every day of my life. I know it's possible because where you are, joy is found. And you are with me. Your Word says it. Your Word is true.

Surprised by Joy

by Sandy Lipsky

You have turned my mourning into joyful dancing. You have taken away my clothes of mourning and clothed me with joy.

PSALM 30:11 (NLT)

MY NIECE PHONED me. This was an unexpected pleasure since we had usually communicated through my sister. The words she spoke to me over the airways sounded like the rustling of colorful leaves on a brilliant autumn afternoon and smelled like baby powder.

"I'm pregnant."

I couldn't contain the tears raining down my cheeks. My heart felt like a balloon on the verge of bursting. Amid the stifled screams of celebration, I blurted, "Congratulations!"

Our family was in the valley of grief. Only a few months prior, my mom had passed away. Her absence left a huge hole. I thought of the goodness of the Lord. He sent us a blessing in the middle of our sorrow.

Questions replaced rejoicing months later when an ultrasound revealed the precious little one would be born with Down syndrome. I believe in the goodness of God, but this diagnosis felt like a punch to the gut. My usually happy self plummeted into a dark state. Jeremiah in the Bible sounded more hopeful than me. But a friend overheard my laments one day and shined a flashlight on my gloom. She shared, "Someone in our church has Down syndrome, and she brings me so much happiness."

In a quiet moment of reflection, I wondered if this extra chromosome could be a gift given to a chosen few. Did it contain an added dollop of joy?

My grandniece is now a toddler. Because we live eight hundred miles away, I jumped at the chance to watch her when asked during a recent holiday. We laughed and played together for hours. Fun-loving, sensitive, and creative describe her personality. And when she called me by name, it tasted delicious, like eating a cinnamon roll smothered in frosting. My friend was right, and so was God. My mourning turned into joy.

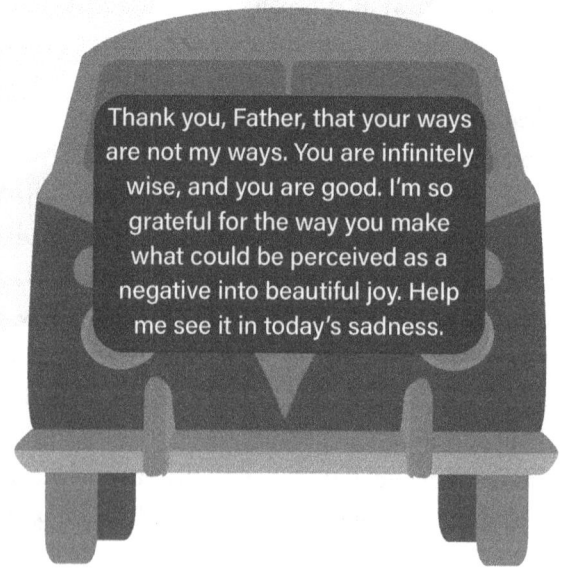

Thank you, Father, that your ways are not my ways. You are infinitely wise, and you are good. I'm so grateful for the way you make what could be perceived as a negative into beautiful joy. Help me see it in today's sadness.

It's Snow Problem, Mom!

by Lisa-Anne Wooldridge

You make known to me the path of life; in your presence there is fullness of joy; at your right hand are pleasures forevermore.

PSALM 16:11 (ESV)

I GRABBED THE WALL to steady myself as my mind struggled to take in the scene before me. I'd been in the kitchen putting away groceries while my children napped—or so I thought. Now, I saw that the entire room had been decorated by my three-year-old, who had somehow managed to open a giant bag of pancake mix from the warehouse store. Every surface was covered with powder—heaps and mounds of it. In the middle of it all stood my precious boy with a look of delirious pride and happiness. I pressed my hand to my face. *Oh, my.*

"Snow!" He smiled up at me and threw two fat handfuls of powder into the air.

Indeed. It was a veritable winter wonderland. The day before, we'd been playing with snow globes at the toy store, each shake of the crystal ball eliciting gales of laughter from my son. He'd been a preemie with health issues and still struggled to communicate, but *snow* was loud and clear and zinged my heart with a happy shock.

My son had transformed our living room because he remembered joy. I closed my eyes and reached for my own joy. I had to swerve around a wall of aggravation and a pothole of dismay to get there, but I made it. My happy place is in God's presence—God is love, but I think he's also joy, and the fruit of the Spirit is his fruit, not ours.

I always imagined the fruit of the Spirit like a farmer's market, with fresh, ripe fruit in overflowing baskets—a riot of colorful and beautiful produce. Joy was waiting for me like a summer peach with a juicy, flavor-filled explosion inside. There is no room for anger or grumpiness when you fill up on joy.

"You made it snow!" I tried to match his excitement.

I picked up my darling boy and swung him in a circle, peppering his face with kisses as he giggled. There'd be time for cleaning up the mess later, time to teach responsibility, and time for a bath. But in the moment, to be present with God meant choosing joy.

When you find yourself in a situation that makes you want to go to your happy place, head straight for the feast that God has already spread and fill up on the good stuff. Taste joy and see how good God is!

Thank you, smiling Father, for being our source, for filling us with the fruit of your Spirit, and for keeping us in the presence of joy!

Dawn Is Breaking

by Diana Leagh Matthews

Weeping may tarry for the night, but joy comes with the morning.
PSALM 30:5 (ESV)

PAIN OVERWHELMED ME. Not physical but emotional pain. Years of abuse scarred my heart and mind. Regrets and woulda, shoulda, coulda tormented me.

I tried to escape my wounds and throw myself into work and busyness, but the lasting memories and regrets only grew heavier.

Finally, I cried out to the Lord, "I can't do this anymore! Will this pain ever end? Help me, Lord. What do I do?"

Depression, fear, and anxiety had become my constant companions. No matter how much I tried, I could not shake them off. I couldn't take the negative thoughts, lingering cynicism, and hopelessness any longer. There was so much more to life that I craved, and I longed to be free of these emotional chains.

On my forty-fifth birthday, I prayed, "Lord, please transform my life. By my fiftieth birthday, make me into the woman you'd have me to be. Help me find the joy only you can provide." Then, I named all the areas that were heavy on my heart. While I'd been a Christian for years, I'd tried to change on my own for way too long. Now, it was the Lord's turn to work.

I'm halfway through that five-year period. The Lord has changed my circumstances and my heart in many ways. While I'm not where I want to be by my fiftieth birthday, I can see how far I've come.

I trust the Lord to take care of what is outside of my control and to empower me to do what needs to be done. This includes being honest with myself (which isn't always easy), reciting Scripture when the Enemy creeps up, listening to worship music, sharing with trusted friends, and, of course, praying. Sometimes, it seems I should do more, while at other times, I don't know how I'll ever have the energy to take the next step.

My heart feels lighter. Those chains holding me back are starting to loosen. A bubble of joy springs up from time to time, and I smile. *Ah, that's what joy feels like!*

There's still a long way to go, but light is starting to shine through. Dawn is breaking, and I'm eager for the morning and the Lord's future plans.

Do you have a burden that creates the darkness of night and the tears of sadness? What will help you be greeted by the joy of a new day?

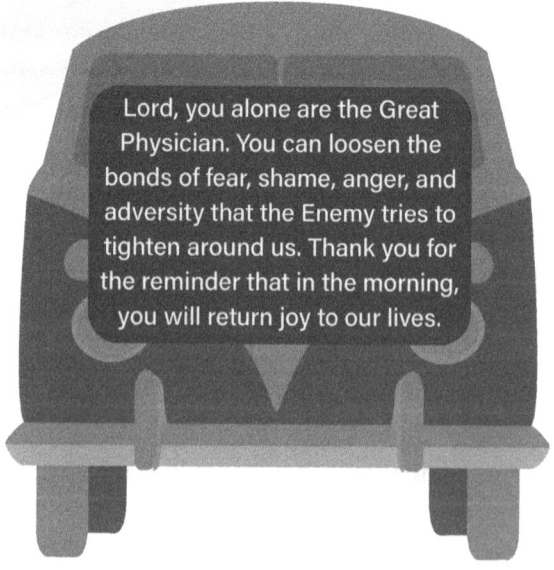

Lord, you alone are the Great Physician. You can loosen the bonds of fear, shame, anger, and adversity that the Enemy tries to tighten around us. Thank you for the reminder that in the morning, you will return joy to our lives.

Glorious, Inexpressible Joy

by Dawn Wilson

Though you have not seen him, you love him. Though you do not now see him, you believe in him and rejoice with joy that is inexpressible and filled with glory.

1 Peter 1:8 (ESV)

*A*FTER A DIAGNOSIS of multiple myeloma, I struggled with depression. Yet, driving down the road one afternoon, I suddenly thought, *Wow! God didn't make just one color of green in his creation!* God's creative paintbox includes both delicate and bold greens: forest green, lime green, olive, emerald, and more. In growing wonder, I noticed many other shades of colors in creation. I prayed with joy, "How much you must love us, Father," and I found myself joyfully loving *him* more.

Most of us remember the excitement of gazing upon something wonderful and finding it difficult to fully express our joy. But to rejoice in something we've never seen? That's another story.

Jesus said the Old Testament patriarch Abraham rejoiced in anticipation of the Messiah's coming. Throughout the psalms, the psalmist rejoiced in God's present and future salvation of his people. Some 500 years before Christ's birth, Zechariah urged God's people to rejoice because their king was coming with salvation. Before the birth of Jesus, his mother, Mary, said her spirit rejoiced in God, her Savior.[a]

---

a   John 8:56; Zechariah 9:9; Luke 1:47

In 1 Peter 1:3–6, Peter wrote to the exiles of the dispersion as they faced various trials, encouraging them to focus on their salvation. Those believers had never personally seen Jesus; yet Peter wrote that they loved Jesus, and their joy was beyond words—inexpressible. In their trials, they trusted and triumphed in God with profound joy that surpassed temporary happiness. It was simply glorious.

Even though Christians today have not seen Jesus in the flesh, our belief in him is not blind faith but, rather, faith based on the biblical record. Paul wrote that more than 500 believers saw the risen Christ at one time. Believers rejoiced in their hope to see the glory of God. Jesus told Thomas that those who had not physically seen him and yet believed were blessed—and part of that blessing was boundless joy.[a]

We may sometimes forget the wonders of our salvation, but the angels don't. They rejoice over every sinner who repents. There is nothing like the extravagant, glorious joy of redeemed sinners who know their names are registered in heaven.[b]

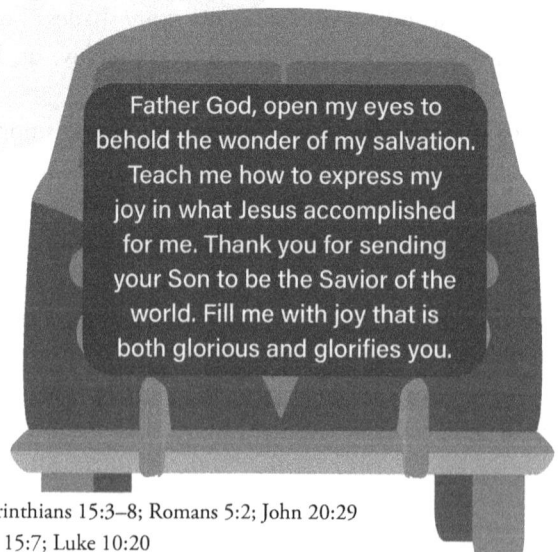

Father God, open my eyes to behold the wonder of my salvation. Teach me how to express my joy in what Jesus accomplished for me. Thank you for sending your Son to be the Savior of the world. Fill me with joy that is both glorious and glorifies you.

---

a   1 Corinthians 15:3–8; Romans 5:2; John 20:29
b   Luke 15:7; Luke 10:20

The Endurance of Joy

by Kathy Carlton Willis

Instead, be very glad—for these trials make you partners with Christ in his suffering, so that you will have the wonderful joy of seeing his glory when it is revealed to all the world.

1 PETER 4:13 (NLT)

WHAT A MIND-BLOWING principle to know that when we suffer, we enter into the fellowship of Christ's suffering. It's one of those join-the-club moments. How can we be very glad when we have trials? By focusing on the wonderful joy of anticipating the glory to come. (I know this because I peeked at the back of the book!)

The word *instead* in the passage indicates that what follows is something that doesn't come naturally to us without God's strength. To be glad during trials—that's not a human trait but a godly one. It's not that we rejoice in the actual trial, but we're glad God never changes, even when circumstances change. We get to abide in him (oh, the blessing of that thought!) rather than sink into our own problems. We are Christ's partners and are assured of seeing his glory.

When troubles come your way, what is your first tendency? To call a friend and vent? To sigh, whine, or cry? To rant with rage? What if you tried to consider it an opportunity to experience great joy? Not just an opportunity for others to observe you reflecting the joy of the Lord, but an opportunity for you to experience such a superhuman emotion, considering the circumstances.

This kind of joy can't be worked up or summoned by your own strength and abilities—it has to start with emptying you of yourself and getting filled up with God's presence. Then he is free to operate in and through you. At that point, the trouble seems less traumatic, and the joy is overwhelmingly magnificent. Such great joy—not merely despite the circumstances but because of them.

Knowing there is wonderful joy ahead assists a sad or mad person in being truly glad. Recognizing there are trials to endure first is more tolerable when we realize it's temporary. What a welcome relief the word *temporary* is. Grandma Mary used to say, "This too shall pass."

I tried saying that during my own trials, but sometimes, the burdens still seemed heavy. Then, I converted the deep concept into a plainer statement (I'm a simple girl who needs simple concepts). Now, I use self-talk such as "It's only temporary." Lightbulb moment: I can endure this because it's not going to last forever. What is in my future is so incredible that I can be truly glad—even before it gets here![2]

> Father, help me experience that wonderful joy even before the fullness of your glory is revealed. It's hard to be part of the suffering club, but it's doable because Jesus partners with me. Thank you for getting it—and getting me! You provide joy despite the trials of life.

Rain Dance

by Lisa-Anne Wooldridge

You have given me greater joy than those who have abundant harvests of grain and new wine.

Psalm 4:7 (NLT)

I HAVE TO CONFESS—I was a chaos gardener before it was trendy on social media. I sowed my first "by faith" seeds as a nine-year-old. My parents wanted to teach me the good lessons of hard work, responsibility, and reward, but I was the poster child for girl-ADHD, so their lesson failed spectacularly.

"It's time to bring in everything left in the garden."

My dad, who was still a little mad that I'd just thrown a few handfuls of seeds willy-nilly into my little corner of the garden and never looked back, gave me a grim smile. "Let's see what you have to show for the seeds I gave you."

I dragged my feet all the way out there and watched in misery as he loaded up the wheelbarrow with the last of his well-manicured harvest. Dread filled me as he strolled over to the weedy patch that was all my own.

"Come over here and pull this one up. It looks like you have a few radishes growing, but don't expect much. The leaves aren't great."

Try as I might, I couldn't pull that radish out of the ground, so he helped me dig it up. It was huge and beautiful. My dad looked annoyed. I took the spade and quickly dug out a dozen more just like it, shouting with joy at each uncovered ruby-red treasure. My dad just rolled his eyes.

"You'd better be glad God watered your garden for you. You didn't even plant those seeds! I don't know how the birds missed them!"

I dug out carrots and radishes enough to fill a basket, each more beautiful than the last, and when finally left alone in my little patch, tears of joy rolled down my face. God had a different lesson in mind for me that summer.

He is faithful when I am not. He is the one who sends the rain and makes the ground good. He's the one who provides. He is the Lord of the harvest.

I did learn to love gardening, tend to growing things, and take joy in pulling weeds and watering. But every time it rains, I feel a surge of gratitude that God is watering my garden. And he has proven himself faithful to send the rain in every season, bringing life and growth for which I could never imagine asking. Pray for rain.

Thank you, Father, for sending the rain to water your garden. With an upturned face and outstretched arms, I gratefully receive the gift of your presence. There is no greater joy.

The Wonder of the Sunrise

by Susan Stitch

Those who live at the ends of the earth stand in awe of your wonders. From where the sun rises to where it sets, you inspire shouts of joy.

PSALM 65:8 (NLT)

BETWEEN THE CHIRPS of nighttime crickets and the sweet songs of early-morning bird calls is a brief moment of expectant silence. The whole earth holds its breath as the first hint of morning reaches out to turn off the stars, one by one. If you wake up early enough, you will slowly see black silhouettes of trees and buildings standing against the horizon.

Birds call to their friends, sharing details of the best breakfast spots. The air is clean and fresh, unhindered by the busyness of the day. A soft breeze tickles the hair on your arms and feels like the pure breath of God. Almost imperceptibly, the colors appear—the dark sky turns purple, and clouds gather the sunbeams and reflect in glorious color.

Watching the sunrise has always been a special time for me. The rest of the world is quiet, and all seems to be at peace before the hectic pace of the day begins. Jesus went out to pray early in the morning, and such morning prayers prime my spirit for the day. God's mercies are new each day as the sun rises, allowing us to put aside the failures of yesterday and move forward with hope for a new day. While we might weep through the night, rejoicing will come in the morning.[a]

As the world slowly comes into focus, I feel deep joy at the vast variety of God's creation. Earth would have been beautiful with just one type of grass, tree, and flower, yet he chose to fill the land with more species and designs than any person could possibly imagine. The wonder of it is more than I can comprehend and brings great joy whenever I contemplate it. Regardless of the continent on which one resides, there is beauty to be found in every corner.

Are you a sunrise person or a sunset person? Both are beautiful and can fill our souls with wonder and inspire shouts of joy. Just don't shout too loudly if you are watching the sunrise—your neighbors who are night owls might not appreciate it!

Heavenly Father, I thank you for the gift of the sunrise. May each new day bring extravagant joy over your creation and thankfulness for your incomprehensible mercy. Let me never take your creation and your love for granted.

a   Mark 1:35: Lamentations 3:22–23; Psalm 30:5

A Heavenly Rejoicing

by Susanne Moore

When they saw the star, they rejoiced exceedingly with great joy.

MATTHEW 2:10 (ESV)

WHEN I WALKED into the hospital room, I was immediately struck by the joy that illuminated my niece Ashley's face. She was cradling the sweetest little ball of pink—her new baby girl. Ever since Ashley was about eight, all I can remember her saying she wanted in life was to get married and have a baby.

After she graduated from college, she moved to Abilene, Texas, and met a handsome fella named Ryan. They married and quickly began trying to start a family. The first few years were rough for them. Ryan had a car accident and was injured, which led to having to file for disability from the military. Ashley had health issues, was diagnosed with celiac disease, had to have her gallbladder removed, and they also tried in vitro fertilization. It just was not happening for them.

One magical day, they saw a "star," a dark pink line on a pregnancy test that brought light into their hard days. Throughout her pregnancy, she struggled, was diagnosed with gestational diabetes, and ultimately had to have an emergency C-section a few weeks early.

Have you ever anticipated a moment of pure, exhilarating excitement in your spirit? The wise men saw the star and rejoiced. Just recognizing that in the sky evoked an elation in their souls.

Finding joy is much deeper than happiness. It's something that encompasses your life. You can have many things going on that are out of your control yet understand God is working in it and through it, and joy will come.

What I saw in that hospital room was the glow of motherhood on her face and her lifelong dream coming true. Pure joy.

The wise men had an even deeper, radical life-changing experience when they saw the star. The anticipation of a Savior and the realization that it was true. Knowing how giving birth to her dream affected Ashley, I find the scope of how the wise men truly felt to be almost unimaginable. Certainly, a heavenly rejoicing for both.

Life can be difficult. Many things get in the way of our hopes and dreams. But God is faithful, he answers prayers, and he certainly brings joy through the many stars that shine bright through the darkness.

Thank you, God, for the heavenly rejoicing and the presence of joy even through the hard things of life. Help me to recognize the star when it appears, reminding me that you are real, and true, and with me.

Joy from the Graveyard

by Beth Jennings Patch

"Just so, I tell you, there is joy before the angels of God over one sinner who repents."

LUKE 15:10 (ESV)

IT WAS 2:00 a.m. when I finished my last drink and shook my head, thinking about the evening's drama. Nothing made sense. The nightclub delivered another evening of alcohol-induced uproars, meaningless conversations, and my emotional outburst of anger at my boyfriend. Disappointed and unhappy, I left alone and staggered across the street to the graveyard.

The moon illuminated the winding road beside the headstones, and my clumsy footsteps zig-zagged far into the cemetery. Tears welled up to overflowing by the time I reached Mom's grave. I stopped and stared at the kind words engraved above her name and dropped to my knees.

"Lord, help me. I've made such a mess of my life," my prayer began. Like a levee breaking, my tears burst into wretched cries and moans of raw, incoherent confessions and pleas for forgiveness. "I don't want to live this way anymore. Please forgive me and change me," I sobbed. My wails broke the silence of the still night as the Lord allowed the graveyard to become the altar on which my life returned to his hands.

If someone had observed the entire scene, they might have assumed I was crazy, drunk, or possessed by a demon. But God and his angels didn't. The Bible says there's joy before the angels of God over a sinner who repents.

That night will always be clear in my mind. I found my rock bottom and returned to my Savior, Jesus Christ.

The next day, I set out on a fresh path of sincerely seeking the Lord. He cleansed the self-destructive behaviors from my life one by one for several years. Since then, I've asked for God's forgiveness countless times and repented of many sins—a regular joy dispenser for the angels, you might say.

When you think of it that way, we can all give the angels reason for joy more frequently. Making things right with God doesn't have to be a massive repentance of a wayward lifestyle. Any and every sin separates us from God, and each one can end with repentance. Then we're reunited with the Lord. It's not only the angels who celebrate with joy when that happens!

Father God, help me live authentically, confessing my sins as they happen and asking for your cleansing power to repent. I love knowing that my repentance brings joy to you and your angels.

Jesus and the Golden Arches

by Stacy Sanchez

I have no greater joy than to hear my children are walking in the truth.

3 JOHN 1:4 (ESV)

*I*T NEVER OCCURRED to me that I would receive a video of my four-year-old grandson taken from inside the restroom of a fast-food restaurant. I can't wait to get videos and pictures of my grandchildren. The more, the better. Blow up my phone with their adorable faces. Yes, please! I have gray hair and wrinkles from raising their parents. I, at least, deserve pictures.

I'm grateful my daughters-in-law frequently bless me with snapshots into their children's lives. I enjoy being involved in my grandcherubs' day-to-day activities. But did I need to be *this* involved?

Unaware his voice was being recorded from the other side of the stall, my grandson joyfully belted out his best version of "Jesus loves me, this I know, for the Bible tells me so"—loud enough that even the customers waiting in line could join in and shout, "Amen!" The restroom walls reverberated with praise. That boy was having church under those golden arches.

I've heard many renditions of this song throughout my life, but listening to my grandson sing it from the bottom of his heart—and lungs—with pure love poured into the words was the most beautiful ever.

Tears ran down my cheeks as I listened to Maverick profess his love for Jesus. My heart leaped for joy because I knew my children, and now my grandchildren, had been taught to walk with the Lord.

No wonder Jesus asked for the little children to come to him.[a] They love him audaciously, without concern for what others think or say.

"I have no greater joy than to hear my children are walking in the truth." In his letter to the early church, the apostle John congratulated his spiritual children for walking in truth amid their trials. His heart overflowed with joy at the reports he received of their persistent faith. Although their faith was tested and tried, the new believers didn't turn away from Jesus. Instead, they drew closer.

Hearing my grandson's proclamation of love for Jesus echoing throughout the fast-food restroom, I understood the apostle John's joy for his spiritual children. I, too, have no greater joy than to know my family walks in truth. Experiencing a grandchild's simple and sincere faith is the best feeling a grandmother can have. It makes the gray hair worth it—sort of.

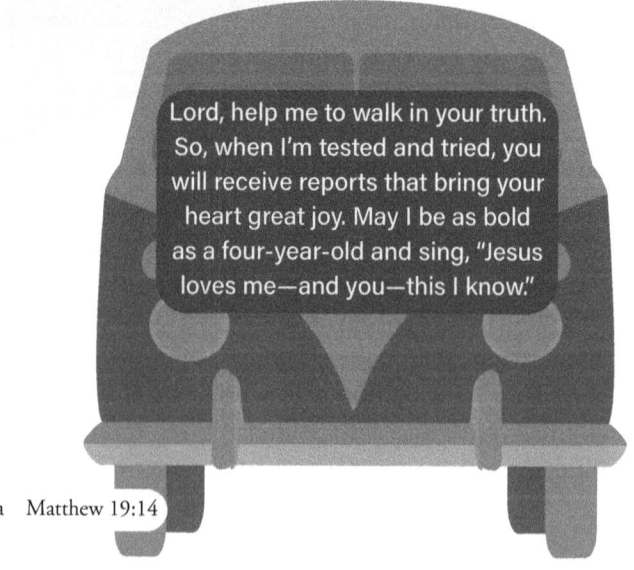

Lord, help me to walk in your truth. So, when I'm tested and tried, you will receive reports that bring your heart great joy. May I be as bold as a four-year-old and sing, "Jesus loves me—and you—this I know."

a   Matthew 19:14

Just Hold Him Tight

by Beth Jennings Patch

"Well done, good and faithful servant. You have been faithful over a little; I will set you over much. Enter into the joy of your master."

MATTHEW 25:21 (ESV)

DIGGING FURIOUSLY IN her carry-on bag, my young granddaughter grabbed the treasure she desperately wanted me to see. "Look, Memaw. I've got Teddy." She pressed the faded pink bear's face gently on my cheek, made a kissing sound, and smiled. Her family had lived overseas for six years, and now that they were back home, she couldn't wait to show me how she'd taken care of the bear.

"Wow! Hi, Teddy," I hugged the skinny, dingy bear with a small rip in his side. "I'm so happy you made it back." My smile was probably as big as hers, if not bigger, as I handed him back.

I remembered what I told her when I gave her the bear. She was only four years old, and they were leaving for Japan the next day, "When you get to missing me, just hold him tight and remember how much I love you."

I could hardly believe how she managed to keep up with Teddy all that time. She slept with him every night—over 2,000 nights. She beat all the odds—six years, four homes, two countries, two younger siblings, and three dogs later—and the bear representing my love for her made it back to the States in one piece. She was determined to keep him close by and protect him.

When I think of all the evenings she laid him beside her and all the times she must have had to rescue this stuffed bear from dogs and siblings, I see her passion. It fills my soul with joy to see her love in such a tangible way. If ever there was an appropriate time to tell someone, "Well done," this is it.

Might this be how Father God feels when he sees us care for gifts he gives us—friends, family, and health, to name a few? I believe every gift he gives us demonstrates his great love for us, and I think I understand why Jesus said, "Enter into the joy of your master." His words paint a picture for us of a smiling and pleased Father.

Oh, Father God, help me treasure your gifts and take good care of them no matter what. I can't wait to hear and see your joy in my faithfulness when I get to my heavenly home.

Artesian Well

by Robin Steinweg

Always be joyful. Never stop praying. Be thankful in all circumstances, for this is God's will for you who belong to Christ Jesus.

1 THESSALONIANS 5:16–18 (NLT)

I WAS A MOODY teen and young adult. I viewed myself in the tragical role of an 1800s Gothic novel heroine, or like Sarah Bernhardt of silent films fame.

In college, this dramatic flair resulted in my playing twelve-year-old Amahl in the opera *Amahl and the Night Visitors*. Amahl, a crippled boy, and his widowed mother are so poor they must start begging. In the night, they are visited by three kings who follow a great star leading them to the baby King of all kings. They bring costly gifts.

While the kings sleep, the mother tries to take one piece of gold that she's certain they wouldn't miss. She is caught. But King Melchior has compassion for her. He says to keep the gold, for the child they seek doesn't need it. His kingdom will be built on love. He will bring us new life—and take our death.

The mother gives back the gold, saying she has waited for such a king all her life. If she weren't so poor, she would send him a gift of her own. Amahl offers his crutch in case the baby might need one. His mother protests. He turns and *walks* to her. God has healed him! Amahl's joy erupts like a geyser. The kings decide to take Amahl with them to bring his crutch and his thanks to the child himself.

At the third performance, during this final scene, the revelation of God's love and forgiveness caused me genuine tears. My heart felt it would burst with joy.

Within a month, a friend shared about Jesus with me, explaining that it's not my behavior that qualifies or disqualifies me for Jesus's gift of salvation, but the gift is based on *his* goodness and sacrificial death on my behalf. Like Amahl, I needed to experience the transformation and respond with joy. And he has never left me.

Since he lives in me, we keep a running conversation. This is prayer. Because of who he is, I know he's working everything out for my good and the good of those I care about. Even if I don't see a happy ending happening, I thank him.

His presence fills me. In him, joy bubbles up like water from an artesian well—just keeps coming and coming. An unlimited overflow of living water, available to everyone. Transformation and healing bring a special kind of joy.

My Lord, I am always joyful, even in sorrow, because you live in me. And in your presence, there is full-out joy. I don't stop praying because you're living with me, and we talk together. You are so, so good to me, regardless of circumstances. I am forever grateful to you!

Joy in the Face of Sorrow

by Joni Topper

So also you have sorrow now, but I will see you again, and your hearts will rejoice, and no one will take your joy from you.

JOHN 16:22 (ESV)

A PHYSICAL THERAPIST SAT on one side of a rectangular table. A patient sat at each end. The therapist worked with me for a few minutes, then turned to work with the other patient.

Nerve damage during carpal tunnel surgery had left me unable to feel three fingers on my right hand. After surgery, I asked my doctor, "How long will it take for the nerves to heal?"

"It takes a while." That answer didn't satisfy me. *Is a while a few weeks, a few months, or longer?*

Sadness and frustration at not being able to feel something grew daily after my surgery. The pros and cons of continuing to play the piano while my hand healed stretched my commitment as the church accompanist. A decision that affected others. Pushing through the awkwardness of not feeling the keys, I realized the importance of the sense of touch. Oddly, the worship music I'd nearly sidestepped played a huge role in stabilizing my joy.

Then, the hand of that other patient at my table came into focus. I'd been wallowing in self-pity. Three of her fingers were gone. She could not look forward to feeling them ever again. A sinking feeling came over me just as the lady looked up. "Fran?" I asked.

"Joni?" she returned the question. My attention to my own sorrow made me temporarily oblivious to her plight. I knew her. We'd been coworkers a few years before.

I realized my sorrow was temporary, but hers was permanent. I looked forward to the day my hand healed. Fran had no hope of her fingers functioning again.

When Jesus told his disciples they would have sorrow, it was the kind of sadness I felt for my loss. Temporary. Their relationship with Jesus ensured that they would only be separated for a while. Knowing the glory of a reunion awaited them changed their ability to persevere through that pain.

I weighed the importance of continuing to serve at the piano—the disciples wrestled with continuing to serve a Savior they could no longer see. Today, we believe in Jesus, whom we have not seen. Then, they believed a man they could see, but only with spiritual eyes could they know he was God. Though they did not fully understand, they trusted Jesus's words that no one could take their joy when they reunited with him.

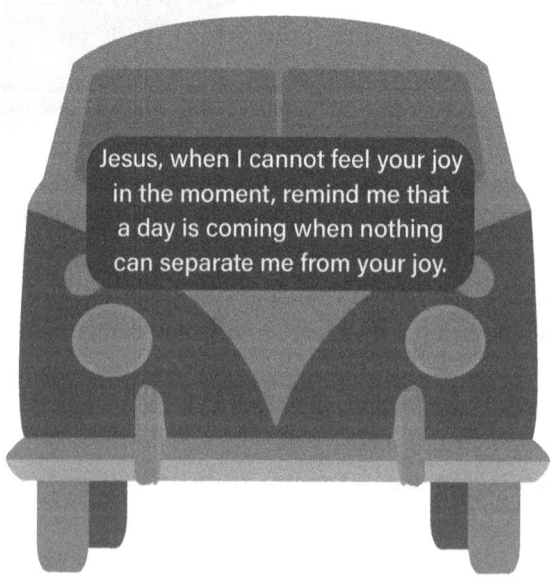

Jesus, when I cannot feel your joy in the moment, remind me that a day is coming when nothing can separate me from your joy.

On the Trail to Joy

by Beth Kirkpatrick

Let us run with endurance the race that is set before us, looking to Jesus, the founder and perfecter of our faith, who for the joy that was set before him endured the cross, despising the shame, and is seated at the right hand of the throne of God.

Hebrews 12: 1–2 (ESV)

WHEN I WAS a girl, my parents took my sister and me on lots of trips to the outdoors. Whether it was a day trip to a favorite picnic spot or a longer camping expedition to another state, we often took hikes to enjoy the natural beauty of our surroundings.

But I wasn't an outdoorsy girl. I preferred to have my nose in a book during the driving part of the outings and frequently complained about the length of the hike, the outside temperature, the steepness of the trail, and anything else that came to mind. I was not always a joyful trail companion.

Once, when I was dragging my feet and whining about when the walk would ever end, my dad made some gentle jesting remark that pricked my pride and my conscience. I quickly flounced ahead of my family, arriving first at the small pond that was our destination. Peeling off my shoes and socks, I sat on a log and dangled my bare feet in the pool. My smug smile of victory became a mask of horror, and I shrieked, "Leeches!" as I kicked and splashed frantically. By the time my family caught up to me, I had managed to fling the slimy critters off and was a very humbled hiker.

Unfortunately, as an adult, I sometimes find myself complaining about my hike through life. I still prefer to have my nose in a book, and parts of the trail leave me sweaty and unsatisfied. Frequently I take matters into my own hands, marching off ahead of my Father. Then I find myself in scary situations, wishing I had not been so quick to wander away.

Hebrews 12:2 helps me understand how to become an accomplished hiker. Jesus is our example of someone who knew how to keep his destination in mind, leaving out all the whining. He endured the most arduous hike up a hill without complaint and achieved the most beautiful view from the right hand of God.

When I'm tempted to complain or hurry off on my own path, I need only fix my eyes on Jesus, knowing that following him leads to true joy.

Dear God, as I hike the trail you have planned for my life, help me to put aside my complaints. May I follow Jesus with a heart full of joy.

The Journey

by Sally Ferguson

Their abundant joy and their deep poverty [together] overflowed in the wealth of their lavish generosity. For I testify that according to their ability, and beyond their ability, they gave voluntarily, begging us insistently for the privilege of participating in the service for [the support of] the saints [in Jerusalem].

2 Corinthians 8:2–4 (amp)

IT'S NOT A good idea to have a laughing fit when you're driving a vanload of women. Believe me, I've tried. My eyes close into slits, and then it's hard to see the white lines on the side of the road. And I'm pretty sure it's important for the chauffeur to have clear vision when the vehicle is in motion.

Silliness abounds when we go on road trips with the gals. We get the giggles when we get away from daily responsibilities. The ride becomes a haven for releasing pent-up emotions and feeling the acceptance of those who love us, even if we've just met. That's what I love about the family of God—a generosity of love overflows to each one in the sisterhood as we find common ground. Those van rides to retreat destinations become holy ground where marriages are affirmed, parenting is reinforced, and heavy hearts are lifted. When we climb out of cramped quarters, we laugh and say, "Let's do it again!"

Isn't it just like our heavenly Father to pair us up for life's adventure on the road toward our heavenly home? He knew we would need traveling buddies to ease travel-weary souls and to help us navigate the bumpy terrain. Sometimes, those gal pals even help us laugh when we most want to cry at the messiness of life. They renew us with the privilege of sharing, caring, and serving each other with a listening ear. The best joyride of all.

> Father, thank you for the rich variety of personalities in our world. Each one is a beautiful reflection of your creative handiwork and thoughtful planning. Help me lavish your love on others and be a good travel buddy on life's journey. May I be a mirror for your reflection to bring overflowing joy to everyone I meet.

No Sing, Mama!

by Missy Eversole

Oh come, let us sing to the LORD; let us make a joyful noise to the rock of our salvation!

PSALM 95:1 (ESV)

GENTLY ROCKING MY eighteen-month-old son, I began talking to him about his little brother, who was due to arrive in a few weeks. Grant's life would change from being an only child to being a big brother. While my husband and I were ecstatic about our new addition, we knew that very soon, we wouldn't have as much one-on-one time with Grant.

Mornings became a treasured time together in the rocking chair. From reading to feeding, the rocker became a place for cuddles and snuggles.

One morning, I began singing. It was a made-up song, not too loud and not too soft. A simple song letting him know how much I loved him. After singing the third verse, Grant's tiny hand pressed against my mouth, and with a mischievous grin, he declared, "No sing, Mama!"

No, sing, Mama?

Who did he think he was? A judge on *American Idol*? Did he not appreciate the "joyful noise" I was making?

With a chuckle, I removed his little hand and started singing again. Grant's hand returned to my mouth, and once again, he said, "No sing, Mama!"

It was a moment that echoed with both the tenderness of motherhood and a reminder of a past wound. My sweet toddler's words transported me back to a time in my childhood when I tried to lead the singing in church, only to be met with a less-than-encouraging response and told to sit down with my classmates.

The memory stung, and self-doubt crept in.

However, remembering the judgmental glances, harsh comments, and the hush of my child's request, I discovered a more profound truth. God doesn't care about the perfection of my voice—he only longs for my genuine praise.

Always remember this timeless truth, "Oh come, let us sing to the LORD; let us make a joyful noise to the rock of our salvation!" If you are like me and can't carry a tune in a bucket, don't let that stop you from rejoicing in the Lord! Praise him for all he has done in your life.

I still sing to Grant. But now I get an eye roll and a chuckle. With the same mischievous smile, my twenty-two-year-old still jokingly says, "No sing, Mama!"

Father, you are the rock of my salvation, and may nothing hold me back from making a joyful noise as I see you at work in my life.

A Tranquil Heart of Joy

by Denise Margaret Ackerman

For he will not often consider the [troubled] days of his life, because God keeps him occupied and focused on the joy of his heart [and the tranquility of God indwells him].

ECCLESIASTES 5:20 (AMP)

WHEN YOU ARE faced with challenging situations, do you struggle to keep a joyful heart? We can learn how to stay close to God during difficult times by studying the book of Daniel. Although a teenager when captured and taken away from everything familiar, Daniel kept his focus on God and remained faithful throughout his life.

Chapter 1 of Daniel sets the scene: Nebuchadnezzar, King of Babylon, besieged and overtook Jerusalem. His army plundered the house of God and captured Israel's finest young men (one of whom was Daniel), demanding they be prepared for service in his palace. The king ordered the captives' names to be changed and the people be assigned a new diet. He demanded the captives to learn the language and literature of the Chaldeans.

Daniel cooperated with these expectations, except when it came to breaking his Jewish upbringing regarding the king's food. Instead, Daniel stayed the course of his upbringing. He purposed in his heart not to defile himself with the king's delicacies or with wine. Although Daniel and fellow captives Hananiah, Mishael, and Azariah avoided the King's rich food, they excelled and rose above those who ate it. God blessed them with knowledge and wisdom, and they were chosen to serve in Nebuchadnezzar's palace.

These young men remained close to God. In chapter 2, we learn that they joined Daniel in prayer, asking God to reveal the meaning of Nebuchadnezzar's disturbing dream. God miraculously provided the interpretation, which temporarily humbled Nebuchadnezzar's heart, leading him to promote Daniel to a high place of authority in Babylon.

Others noticed Daniel's lifelong walk with God. After serving under King Nebuchadnezzar and his successors, Daniel continued serving a fourth ruler, King Darius. "Then this Daniel distinguished himself above the governors and satraps, because an excellent spirit was in him; and the king gave thought to setting him over the whole realm."[a]

This excellent spirit was a result of Daniel's faithful walk with God. Despite being a captive, he accepted his difficult situation and continually focused on serving God—the joy of his heart.

Like Daniel, we can rely on God during trying circumstances. "Rejoice in our confident hope. Be patient in trouble, and keep on praying."[b] God will give us tranquil hearts if we draw close to him in prayer and keep the faith—holding fast to the promises in his Word.

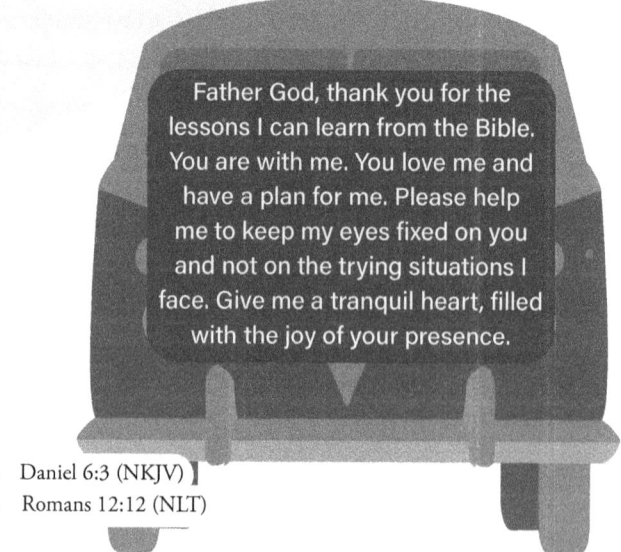

Father God, thank you for the lessons I can learn from the Bible. You are with me. You love me and have a plan for me. Please help me to keep my eyes fixed on you and not on the trying situations I face. Give me a tranquil heart, filled with the joy of your presence.

---

a Daniel 6:3 (NKJV)
b Romans 12:12 (NLT)

Heart Cushions

by Mindy Cantrell

May the God of hope fill you with all joy and peace in believing, so that by the power of the Holy Spirit you may abound in hope.

ROMANS 15:13 (ESV)

WHAT FEELINGS DO the words "filled with joy" inspire in you? Maybe ecstatic happiness? Have you ever experienced that feeling—exhilarating happiness bubbling up inside you? Ah, it feels so good, doesn't it? I loved it! That is, until my beautiful nine-year-old son died tragically in a school bus accident. For me, *all* joy and happiness died with him that day.

How can I ever feel joy again when my whole being is endlessly engulfed in sorrow? I questioned it all. I couldn't understand what God meant in that verse above. My joy was forever buried with my son.

However, in the years since, between bouts of drowning and dog-paddling through grief, I learned there is a difference between joy and happiness. Joy *can* be present in your life, no matter the circumstance.

First, I learned happiness is a feeling. When feel-good things of this earth—good food, good relationships, nice possessions—fill our lives, our brains feel happy and content. But when we lose any of those things, that happiness tends to disappear, doesn't it?

On the other hand, joy is a state of being. Joy comes from *spiritually* good things. Things that hold eternal or everlasting value. Things that cannot be lost. Like the everlasting love God has for each of us. And the knowledge that we will be reunited with our loved ones who have gone on before us when we believe in and have a personal relationship with God. Hope and joy are what God gives us when we love and trust him.

Consider the words of author and pastor Sam Storms, "Joy is not necessarily the absence of suffering, it is the presence of God."[3]

Perhaps Pastor Storms was inspired by the words of King David, "You make known to me the path of life; in your presence there is fullness of joy."[a] Indeed, like King David, I have realized joy is the peaceful assurance in my soul that I am loved by a heavenly Father who created me for good things and is faithful to bring about those good things in my life. Joy is knowing I will see my beautiful little boy, Tommy, again in heaven.

Joy is God's ever-present, hope-filled cushion surrounding our hearts, supplying calm, peace, and comfort, no matter what each day holds. Simply put, true joy is the ever-presence of God in our lives.

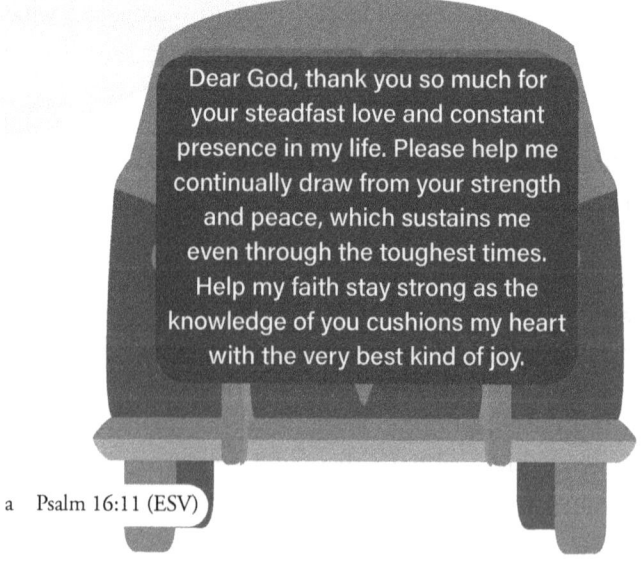

Dear God, thank you so much for your steadfast love and constant presence in my life. Please help me continually draw from your strength and peace, which sustains me even through the toughest times. Help my faith stay strong as the knowledge of you cushions my heart with the very best kind of joy.

[a] Psalm 16:11 (ESV)

Are You Listening?

by Carolyn Gaston

The LORD your God in your midst, The Mighty One, will save; He will rejoice over you with gladness, He will quiet you with His love, He will rejoice over you with singing.

ZEPHANIAH 3:17 (NKJV)

"MOMMY, MOMMY, COME quick! I think I'm going to write a song," our middle daughter said with a giggle. This was not an uncommon occurrence at our house, so I knew exactly what to do. I turned off the burner on the stove, where the spaghetti sauce was simmering, and wiped my greasy hands on my jeans.

I grabbed a pencil and a scrap of paper from the junk drawer in the kitchen and started writing as Stacy sang about sunshine, butterflies, and her love for Jesus and our family. This precious three-year-old had burst into song once again, and for a few magical moments she sang her heart out right in front of my eyes. Even though these sweet memories still bring me lots of happiness, they pale in comparison to the utter joy I feel when I read the words of God to the Old Testament prophet Zephaniah.

What a joy-filled idea—God sang over Jerusalem. Maybe he also sings over me with joy! Just as God reassured Zephaniah, I find assurance in this passage. I cherish that God is with me, and he is mighty to save. How blessed I am that the God of the universe celebrates and sings because of mere mortals. So, I stop and ask, "What is God singing? What is the tune of his song?"

Perhaps it's a lullaby telling me I have peace in his presence. Maybe he shouts an upbeat song, reminding me that I am his child. Could it be a classical symphony where God declares his deep, everlasting love for me? Is he calling me the apple of his eye? Or perhaps he is promising to bring me out of darkness into his marvelous light. Is he voicing verses of victory for me?

While I've never actually heard any glad shouts or tender melodies of mercy coming down from heaven, I can absolutely imagine God calling my name and quieting me with his love. So many times in the book of Psalms, we read about God's people shouting songs of joy to worship him, but the thought of God himself shouting and rejoicing over me is humbling. The eternal God is joyful when he sings over me. How very blessed I am! Do I hear him? Am I listening? And you? Do you hear him? Are you listening?

Mighty God, I thank you for quieting me with your love and singing joyful songs because of me.

Gathering the Harvest of Joy

by Edna Earney

Those who sow in tears shall reap with shouts of joy!

PSALM 126:5 (ESV)

ONE TYPICAL MORNING, this young mother stood at her kitchen sink and surveyed her situation. She faced a day's worth of milk-encrusted bottles that needed sterilizing for the baby on her hip. Toys lay scattered across the kitchen and living room floors, where two toddlers tussled over the same doll. The trash overflowed, and she could smell the latest diaper added to the top. She thought, "Two in diapers, two who can't dress themselves, one still on the bottle. I'm going to wash bottles and change diapers for the rest of my life."

A bit dramatic, I know. But that was my literal thought that day. My brain knew this was a season of life, but my emotions led me to wonder if I would ever again sit down for a second without first wiping three noses. I was prone to think often of the B.C. days, Before Children, when my hubby and I felt free enough to hop in the car for an unplanned trip with only an overnight bag. A trip out of the house now meant a car trunk crammed with supplies.

The Israelites whom the psalmist wrote about in Psalm 126 first recalled their days of blessings from God, days of laughter and joy. But then their situation changed because they next asked for their fortunes to be restored. They had become captives, and they no longer felt bathed in blessings. But they knew the source of their joy and believed this season would pass. They sang this truth: if they remained faithful in this season of captivity, if they sowed good seed even in their sadness, the joy-filled harvest would eventually come.

Likewise, common sense told me the toddler season would pass. I'd sacrifice some spontaneity and time to myself, but that sacrifice had a purpose. And my mothering heart knew I had important seeds to plant right then, seeds God intended to harvest for his good purposes in his timing. I found joy in my purpose.

Now in our silver-haired years, my husband and I reflect on those days of parenting toddlers with a knowing nod to the passing seasons of life and a fuller understanding of God's harvest. We rejoice in our grown children and our grandchildren. We urge them to faithfully plant good seeds. And we commit them to the joy-filled future God has for them and for all believers.

Dear God, you establish the seasons of my years and ask for my faithfulness regardless of the season. Help me to remain faithful even when I'm sad. Lead me to see joy in the purpose of every season, knowing I will have eternal joy with you.

God Delights in Me

by Robin Steinweg

The LORD's delight is in those who fear him, those who put their hope in his unfailing love.

PSALM 147:11 (NLT)

IN MY EARLY twenties, I came into a relationship with Jesus Christ. Until then, I had shown the world fake joy. A smiling face hid the dislike I felt for people who were mean or snobbish. I lived with fear, convinced I wasn't good enough for heaven and terrified of dying before I was ready to be good enough. Then, a friend shared that Jesus was the only one good enough, and he paid for my sin with his own perfect life.

The moment I tasted his forgiveness, joy filled me. The real deal! It never diminished because he never left me, and he is the source of that joy.

Years later, one January, a friend challenged me to choose a word to be my focus for the year. I knew it had to be joy. That entire year, I saw or heard the word *joy* everywhere. In stores, in my reading, in sermons, and in conversations, there it was again. I reveled in it. I looked up Bible verses with the word *joy*. That year was about the joy I experienced in Christ, which I hoped to reflect to others.

The next year, my chosen word was *delight*. I didn't forget joy; I just added delight to my focus. Again, I looked up Bible verses that included the word *delight*.

One night, I attended a service of prayer and praise. I sang along with the worship band, enjoying God's presence, when words impressed themselves boldly on my mind and heart. Was I hearing them? They seemed louder than the music, and I sat unaware of anything or anyone around me.

"You've had it wrong, you know," I heard. "The greatest thing is not the joy or delight you have in me." He had my full attention. "It's how much joy and delight *I* take in *you*, my precious child."

I remain in awe over that night and those words from Jude even years later. As if forgiveness, eternal life, and unfailing love weren't enough—he also delights in me!

And this includes you, too, my sister or brother in Christ. You too.

My Savior, my King, how is it possible that you could find joy and delight in me? Yet your Word says it, so I must believe it. I will spend eternity in awe of it. Grateful. Awed by your love.

Restore My Joy

by Pattie Reitz

*Restore to me the joy of your salvation, and
make me willing to obey you.*

PSALM 51:12 (NLT)

CERTAIN TIMES OF the year are naturally more joyful than others. Special occasions and holidays are cheerful celebrations that bring joy and happiness to our hearts. When celebrating with my family, I feel content with a sense of fulfillment and joy settling deep in my heart.

However, what about the times when joy seems fleeting and hard to find? When life happens, and stress steals our peace? Are you like me and wonder where your joy is hiding?

When I feel like that—as if something is missing—I usually turn to God's Word to figure out what it is. The Bible tells us that the joy of the Lord is our strength.[a] And while that is true, of course, it doesn't always *feel* true.

Psalm 51:12 adds a little more to the joy conversation. The verse begins, "Restore to me the joy of your salvation," and I pray, *Okay, Lord, thank you for your salvation. Can you please restore joy to my heart?* But the next part is a bit harder: "and make me willing to obey you."

Whoa, there; slow your roll, psalmist. What do you mean, obey?

---

a Nehemiah 8:10

I obey! Well, most of the time. Much of the time. In all honesty, I *try* to obey—and when I know what I have done wrong, I pray and confess my wrongs to make things right with my Lord.

Obedience means more than just putting a checkmark on a list of things I've done right, though. I wonder, is the word *restore* in the verse what I need to focus on instead of a list of laws? Restoring relationships, restoring trust, restoring my faith in Christ. If I do what I can to restore what is out of place with an obedient heart, then God says he will restore my joy.

Does God's promise to restore joy sound as wonderful to you as it does to me? While I wish I could say with certainty that if you do this, you'll automatically find joy, I cannot make that promise. But God can and does restore our joy regardless of our incomplete checklists.

Dear Lord, thank you for giving me occasions for joy, and grace for the less joyful moments. Thank you for helping me find joy in obeying your Holy Word each day. Help me to encourage others, and please restore our joy as we seek to obey your Word.

Spilling Over with Joy

by Denise Margaret Ackerman

*Then the trees of the forest will sing for joy before the
LORD; For He comes to judge and govern the earth.*

1 CHRONICLES 16:33 (AMP)

"GRANNY, GRANNY, *GRANNY!*" Ricky* squealed, as he scrambled across his daddy's lap, out of the still-running truck, and into my outstretched arms.

"Oh buddy, I missed you so much," I exclaimed, as I carried him into our house—his body trembling with excitement.

It had been several weeks since Ricky had spent time with us, and I was overjoyed that he had missed me, like I had missed him. Entering the kitchen, I chuckled as he kicked off his boots, sending them in different directions across the room. The moment I removed his winter coat, he grabbed my hand and led me through the house, making a full inspection of everything that had changed since his last visit. It was almost Christmas, and I had recently brought out colorful decorations.

Ricky chattered away, commenting on each item he recognized from the previous year's holiday trimmings. He sought out and switched on every lighted decoration and couldn't wait to press the play button on our vintage reindeer that sings "Jingle Bell Rock."

Once every Christmas light had been lit, Ricky exhaled a deep breath and joined me in my cozy blue recliner. Snuggled together beside the warm glow of the Christmas tree, we shared a sweet conversation about his list for Santa.

Our visit was short—his dad returned to take him home less than an hour after his impromptu arrival. My heart had been stirred by Ricky's exuberant emotions, and it took me a while to regain my composure after they departed. In all my years of life, no one had ever been so excited to see me that they quaked with joy.

As a follower of Jesus, I look forward to the day when I will see my Lord face to face. But I question—am I as excited about that day as I could be? Will I quake with joy, like Ricky did when he saw me? I love our devotional passage in *The Message* paraphrase. "Let Ocean, all teeming with life, bellow, let Field and all its creatures shake the rafters; Then the trees in the forest will add their applause to all who are pleased and present before God—he's on his way to set things right!"[a]

When I consider all the wondrous things my Savior has done for me, my joyful anticipation should be much greater than that of creation. Our Savior is coming again! Let us rejoice and be glad as we await that glorious day.

*Name changed.

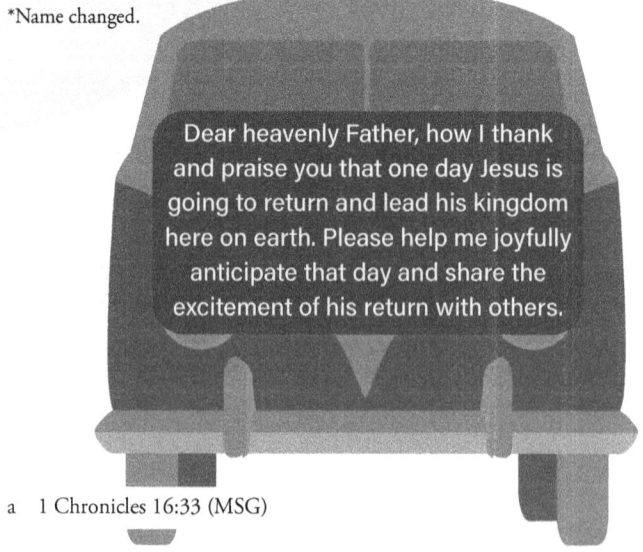

Dear heavenly Father, how I thank and praise you that one day Jesus is going to return and lead his kingdom here on earth. Please help me joyfully anticipate that day and share the excitement of his return with others.

a   1 Chronicles 16:33 (MSG)

Front Porch Storytelling

by Lisa-Anne Wooldridge

I have taken Your testimonies as a heritage forever, For they are the joy of my heart.

Psalm 119:111 (AMP)

I LET THE SCREEN door slam behind me as I ran outside, twirling in my grandmother's yellow chiffon nightgown with pink ribbon roses. It was twilight, and all the folks were settling on the front porch. I waved to my great-grandmother as she sat in her rocking chair in front of the little house across the street. Supper was over, the dishes were done, and it was time for storytelling.

What wild story will Aunt Teen tell this time?

"She looks like your Mama Lauree." Aunt Teen nodded in my direction.

I'd never met my other great-grandmother, but I'd heard she had honey-colored hair and big green eyes like mine. My grandmother smiled her sweet, quirky smile.

"But she takes after Memaw Samples. She's a right handful." Everyone laughed while I scowled.

Fine. If I'm so much like her, then maybe I should sit on her porch. I jumped down and scuffled across the street in my borrowed slippers to my great-grandmother. I put my nose in the air and ignored the hoots of laughter that followed me.

Memaw Samples was a legend. She was quite elderly, but she was just as feisty as she'd ever been. Quick-witted, she could put you in your place in a heartbeat, but she was also funny, warm, and compassionate. She was known for borrowing her grandson's motorcycles and riding them through town at the age of eighty and getting stuck high up in a tree trying to get a cat down a few years later. The stories she shared about the characters in our family fascinated me.

She told of ancestors who were preachers, politicians, and outlaws, but through it all, she wove a narrative of God's goodness, faithfulness, and love. Wherever God intersected with our story, grace abounded. I learned his name was above all names on our family tree. She told me I was the next chapter in her God story and that my children and grandchildren would be the next chapters in mine if I sat on the porch and kept the story alive.

I'm on my patio now with all the kids around the firepit. It's story time.

Father of our family, help us to remember all the wonderful things you've done for us as we pass our stories down and keep your Word alive for the next generation. May our testimonies bring joy to our children forever!

Peace

Peace Chips

by Sandy Lipsky

"God blesses those who work for peace, for they will be called the children of God."

MATTHEW 5:9 (NLT)

I LIKE TO BE liked. When I sense someone does not enjoy my presence, it causes chaos in my soul. Because I crave peace, an internal battle ensues until harmony is achieved.

After college, I began working as a registered nurse at a local hospital in Wisconsin. I preferred the night shift and quickly settled into a routine. Friendships with my coworkers came easy—with all but one. The charge nurse for our shift did not like me. It became embarrassingly obvious. When I entered the breakroom, Sue* left. Her eyes narrowed, and her mouth contorted into a scowl when I greeted her with a cheerful smile and hello. I learned to give her a wide berth in the hallway and to keep my head down as she passed.

This avoidance behavior continued for over a year. Tired of the daily dodge, I knew I had to work on my relationship with her. Sue was an excellent nurse whom I respected. Efficient and dependable. Doctors and nurses alike trusted her judgment. She seemed to be a constant figure on the obstetrics floor. Sue deserved honor not evasion.

"Where's Sue?" I asked after not seeing her for days.

"Vacation," a fellow employee responded.

My nemesis ended up being gone for several weeks. Although I welcomed the reprieve, I started to become concerned. Like the Grinch whose heart grew—my heart softened. In my quiet time, I began to ask the Lord how to serve Sue. After a week of prayer, I had a plan. Chips. Each workday during break, Sue ate potato chips. With a *welcome back* note taped to a bag of crisps, I left the peace offering in my locker. My preparation paid off when she returned to the hospital a few days later. While Sue busied herself with a delivery, I snuck the gift into our breakroom.

We did not become *besties* after that day, but things changed. She no longer left the room when I arrived. Her facial features softened when she looked at me, and at times, we even had one-on-one conversations. The modest gift of chips gave birth to a big reward. Peace. I welcomed its arrival.

*Name changed.

> Peace is a wonderful gift in a relationship. Thank you for softening my heart and helping me see Sue as you do. Father, you are creative and wonderful. You knew just what my coworker needed, and I'm grateful you gave me the courage to act on your idea.

Learning to Live Peaceably

by Betty Predmore

*If it is possible, as much as depends on you,
live peaceably with all men.*

ROMANS 12:18 (NKJV)

SPOILING FOR A good fight used to be second nature to me. Having grown up in an environment where anger was demonstrated freely, animosity was my go-to response for most negative situations. After all, that was what I was accustomed to. It was my rendition of normal.

Sadly, I was setting the same example for my children. From one generation to the next, I followed the pattern and allowed anger to be passed down, spurring it on like a clown in front of a rodeo bronc.

God had to do a huge amount of work in me before I could face this issue head-on, not in my own strength, but in his. I remember a particular time of Bible reading when I came across Romans 12:18. It basically said to me that I cannot control the way other people act, but I can certainly be more responsible with my own behavior. I can choose to be peaceable, even if it is not reciprocated.

This revelation did not bring about instantaneous change. It showed me that I had a choice to make. I could either continue to model poor behavior to my children or intentionally put the hard work into changing my responses. Then, I would show them that there are alternate ways to respond to people and that people can change when they look to God for strength.

In my heart, I was so filled with shame for my actions, and had a great desire to improve.

That tug in my heart came many years ago. Since then, I have spent countless hours talking to God and asking him to mold me into a better example for those watching. God has been so good to me, allowing me the opportunity to grow and change, becoming a better example of a Christ follower with each passing year.

Anger has not left me entirely in the dust. It presents itself time and again. I have learned that grace and compassion go a lot further than angry words and hostility. Peace is the answer, and whenever possible, that is the route I choose to take.

I am grateful that God knew my heart and heard my prayer to be at peace with others. It has profoundly changed my life, not to mention the lives of those I hold most dear. I can never thank him enough for the gift of peace.

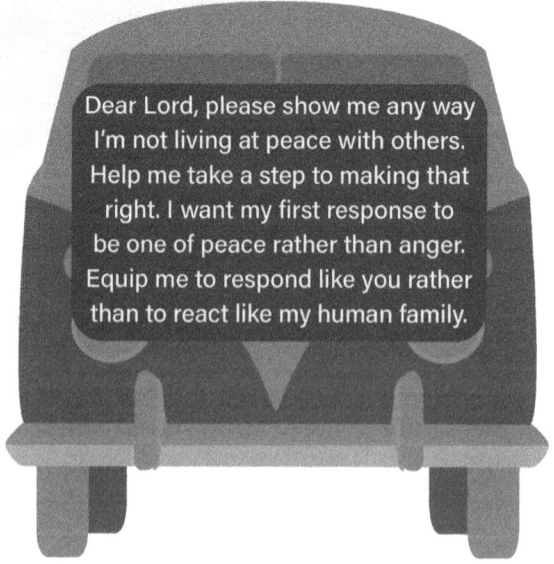

Dear Lord, please show me any way I'm not living at peace with others. Help me take a step to making that right. I want my first response to be one of peace rather than anger. Equip me to respond like you rather than to react like my human family.

Learning to Love Peace

by Kathy Carlton Willis

But the wisdom from above is first of all pure. It is also peace loving, gentle at all times, and willing to yield to others. It is full of mercy and the fruit of good deeds. It shows no favoritism and is always sincere.

JAMES 3:17 (NLT)

WHAT DO YOU suppose having a pure heart has to do with our pursuit of peace? This passage says it leads to wisdom from above—godly wisdom. This same wisdom has several other traits mentioned. Which of these do you find the most difficult to put into practice?

Maybe I'm in love with the idea of peace more than the work of peace. It takes a village to help me pursue the God of peace above all things. My whole life has led me to this point. It feels like self-harm to identify the immature selfish passions I struggle with. But so necessary in order to remove them. And when I deal with some, more pop up!

"Run from anything that stimulates youthful lusts. Instead, pursue righteous living, faithfulness, love, and peace. Enjoy the companionship of those who call on the Lord with pure hearts."[a]

These struggles I'm supposed to run from—they include anything I desire that takes me further away from God and distracts from spiritual growth. The best way I've found to run away from them is to run to Jesus.

---

a   2 Timothy 2:22 (NLT)

As I switch gears and think of the opposite list, I have a better action plan. How does pursuing righteous living, faithfulness, love, and peace help me to mature as a believer? I'm going to chase after these things!

The passage above encourages us to enjoy the companionship of others who have pure motives in seeking the Lord. Fellowship with other Christ followers helps us stay focused on godly actions and attitudes as we desire to grow in the Lord. *The Message* paraphrase words the last part this way: "joining those who are in honest and serious prayer before God."

Who in your life calls on the Lord with pure hearts? I enjoy interacting with those who practice honest and serious prayer. (While I'm not with them when they're alone with God, I can see his God-shine on them.) They are the ones who help me pursue peace and provide an environment conducive to peace.

Pursue others who pursue peace, and you'll be well on your way to having more peace in your life![4]

Father, peace seems far away when I've surrounded myself with people who hurt me. And when I pursue goals that seek selfish gain, I miss out on you. But when I seek the company of those who seek you, I find peace. And when I pursue you, I find peace. I know these things! Help me to do them today.

Just Pray

by Susan Stitch

I pray that God, the source of hope, will fill you completely with joy and peace because you trust in him. Then you will overflow with confident hope through the power of the Holy Spirit.

Romans 15:13 (NLT)

I AM NOT VERY eloquent when I pray. If I'm honest, I frequently fall asleep during bedtime prayers (hmm, maybe I shouldn't pray while lying down). In addition, I can act like a petulant five-year-old reciting a birthday wish list—God, please heal this friend, bless that one, and grant me what I really want. There are even times when I start a prayer with a request and then stop, remembering I should probably thank God for his blessings before I place my order.

The apostle Paul, on the other hand, authored prayers that I copy and post on my wall. The prayers in his letters are full of prose that demonstrates God's awesome love and power. Each prayer is a complete lesson in itself—telling the wonders of God, requesting the gifts we should seek, providing advice on our roles, and listing the benefits to be gained.

Romans 15:13 is one of my favorite prayers. Can you imagine being filled completely with joy and peace? To me, joy is often a choice—relying on God and reflecting his love to the world. Peace, on the other hand, can be impossible for me to attain without heavenly assistance. The craziness of the world, difficulties with relationships, and personal struggles consort together to take away any tranquility I feel.

But Paul takes it one step further. Joy and peace are not the end goal of the prayer. Joy comes from the anticipation of seeing our hopes fulfilled, and peace comes from the assurance that God will fulfill those hopes.[5] These result in a level of hope for a future that will help us get through any trial as we rest in the power of the Holy Spirit.

Thankfully, I don't have to be articulate or even creative when I pray. God just wants me to talk to him, tell him my troubles, and thank him for his gifts. I can read the prayers of others, and they are just as meaningful today as they were originally. Or I can simply cry out in pain, frustration, or joy, and the words have the same result. God hears our prayers, honors our intentions, and responds in his time and his way for our good. Whatever we do, just pray!

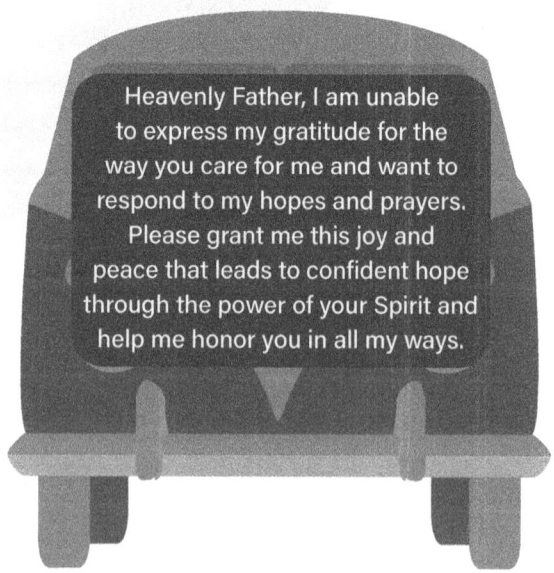

Heavenly Father, I am unable to express my gratitude for the way you care for me and want to respond to my hopes and prayers. Please grant me this joy and peace that leads to confident hope through the power of your Spirit and help me honor you in all my ways.

Facets of Friendship

by Joanie Shawhan

Turn away from evil and do good. Search for peace, and work to maintain it.

Psalm 34:14 (NLT)

FRIENDS ARE LIKE precious jewels in a treasure chest. Each is different—a different color, a different cut, a different shape. Some gems are hard, while others are soft. Some transparent, others opaque. Some jewels are bold and brash, others muted, softer, less noticeable.

But sometimes, we lose our appreciation for these special gems.

I remember one evening when I met a friend for dinner. As we talked about current events, I realized our opinions were diametrically opposed to one another. I froze. How could this be? We both believed in Jesus and his Word. Would I argue and defend my position in hopes of changing her opinion? No. Our friendship was more important than our viewpoints.

We laid aside our preconceived ideas and opinions and pursued the person who unites us—Jesus. We shared what God was doing in our lives and how he was speaking to us. What a welcome conversation to share the way we each experienced a more intimate presence of God in our lives.

Later that evening, I marveled at how God turned a potentially volatile conversation into a deepening friendship through our shared life with him.

I experienced one of the most in-depth times of sharing with my friend. We had let go of our differences and pursued peace. That night, I discovered a new facet of friendship, a side that reflected the light of Christ in a way I had not seen before.

When in conflict, we lost our luster, but when we focused on Jesus, we reflected his light.

Lord, please help me pursue peace when I sense potential conflict. Remind me that my friends are gifts you have placed in my life. Precious jewels, reflecting your light.

Heaven's Morning Light

by Becki James

"Because of God's tender mercy, the morning light from heaven is about to break upon us, to give light to those who sit in darkness and in the shadow of death, and to guide us to the path of peace."

LUKE 1:78–79 (NLT)

I WAITED IN DARKNESS. Dew clung to everything with a dense fog. I tugged my sleeves, stretching them over my palms, but even they felt saturated. I pressed my grip firmer around the hot mug. Steam rose, mingling with each exhale. Not a sound. No songbirds. No breeze. Nothing. I shifted to one side, then the other. Darkness had its own voice—quiet and obtrusive. The longer I sat, the louder the invasive thoughts became. I wanted nothing more than to go back inside.

No. Wait it out.

The minutes dragged. "Humph," I grunted at the shadows, "Life is like you—vague and devoid of clarity." The hot sting of tears simmered in the corners of my eyes. I pinched them tight, not wanting to cry again.

"Stay," a soft voice spoke within me.

Releasing the ache, I opened my eyes, and the tears fell. The first sliver of daybreak glinted through the barren branches. A gentle wind rustled my hair, lifting the heavy moisture of twilight. The brightness grew. Pink. Orange. White. All radiating the authority of the rising sun. Dawn had broken free. The night was no more.

Waiting for answers sometimes mirrors anticipating the

dawn. The haze of confusion swells to seismic proportions, shutting out hope and stealing peace. Have you been there? In a place where night never seems to end? Recently, I found myself stuck in the agony of regurgitated prayers. No answers came. Questions piled high. I started to fixate on the problems instead of the basis of my help.

When I am faced with darkness, a light source is pivotal. A match. A lamp. The sun. But what about circumstantial blackness? What about disappointment, discouragement, depression, or despair? God is my source of vitality. Because I have trusted Jesus as my Savior, he lives within me. He never leaves, and he gives me strength. When I acknowledge God is with me, a switch flips in me. My perspective changes—darkness diminishes.

God's mercy is tender. Not only does he see my pain, but he also wants me to dwell in peace. Confidence in him is like knowing the sun is still there. He is faithful to love and lead me as sure as the dawn of each new day. The path to peace illuminates in the presence of my Savior, Jesus Christ. Heaven's morning light breaks upon me with peace.

Lord, thank you for being my Light. There is no darkness that prevails against the power of your presence. Thank you for loving me and leading me to paths of peace.

Nunc Dimittis

by Beth Kirkpatrick

"Lord, now You are letting Your servant depart in peace, According to Your word; For my eyes have seen Your salvation Which You have prepared before the face of all peoples, A light to bring revelation to the Gentiles, And the glory of Your people Israel."

LUKE 2:29–32 (NKJV)

HAVE YOU EVER prayed for something for many years and at last received an answer to your prayers? This is the incredible situation in which Simeon found himself. A just and devout man, he had received a revelation from the Holy Spirit that he would not die until he had seen the Messiah. When Joseph and Mary came to the temple with their infant son, Simeon took Jesus in his arms and blessed God.

His next words have come to be known as the *Nunc dimittis*, which means "now let depart."[6] Simeon not only recognized God's gift to Israel but openheartedly declared the light to be for all people. Since his faithful prayers had been answered, he was ready to depart peacefully.

Simeon's words have been set to music and sung as part of church services for hundreds of years. (Many versions are available online.) Traditionally sung toward the end of the service, these simple words express a deep confidence in God's promises and work among his people, inspiring a profound sense of peace. From simple canticles to intricate organ and choir scores to more modern arrangements, the Nunc dimittis continues to be a resonant theme for God's people—we seek to hold God's peace in our hearts.

As a girl trying to follow the order of service in the hymnal, I remember thinking this song was difficult to sing because it was arranged as a canticle in our liturgy. Some words had their own notes, and some phrases were sung on one tone. But singing this Scripture on many Sundays throughout my childhood implanted it in my memory and in my heart.

Hearing Simeon's words of gratitude, we can imagine the flood of emotion he felt as his most fervent prayer was answered. Simeon was now filled with an overwhelming sense of peace, his long wait finally over. What a blessing for him to have held the Savior in his arms, and what a blessing for us to read his story and share in his peace!

Dear God, thank you for keeping your promise to send a Savior to our world. Help us experience your peace as we, like Simeon, turn our hearts to the light of Jesus.

Did You Say Peas or Peace?

by Joni Topper

"Glory to God in the highest, And on earth peace, goodwill toward men!"

Luke 2:14 (NKJV)

***W**HIRLED PEAS. THAT'S what I want.*
The bumper sticker on the car in front of me transported me back to those beauty pageants I watched with bated breath as a little girl. It seemed as though every beauty queen interview included the words "world peace." Now, as an adult, I giggled at the memory. World peace. That's hardly the same as whirled peas.

"What are you laughing at, Mom?" My six-year-old daughter Crystal asked from the back seat. How could I explain the humor without minimizing the meaning of God's declaration on that starry night? My very favorite bumper sticker of all time said *Spellers of the World Untie!* The humor of that one would be hard to explain to a child for whom spelling was an emerging skill too.

"Remember when Dad told you we were having 'mediocre' for supper and that it was meat and okra?"

"Yes. He was just pulling my leg and trying to confuse me with words that sound like one thing but mean something else." Crystal always knew when we were joking around, even if she did not know what we meant.

"I was laughing at a bumper sticker that did the same thing. Do you remember when the angels spoke to the shepherds the night Jesus was born and announced 'Peace, goodwill toward men'? What do you think that means?"

"I think peace means people are not fighting. I think goodwill means someone wants good things for you."

We were on the right track; now if I could help her understand how these words tied to good tidings from the angel, we'd be getting somewhere. "If I put an ice cube in the setting for a diamond ring, it would be clear and shiny and pretty to look at, but it would melt. The words on the bumper sticker were like ice. But if I put a diamond in that same ring, it would stand the test of time and remain beautiful, right? Those words from the angel that night to the shepherds were like diamonds. They held great value and purpose. Because God sent his son Jesus, we can have peace. Peace has a value that will stand the test of time even more than a diamond."

Father, help me to remember what has value and what does not. Help me to recognize the value of the peace you offer. Help me to embody your timeless peace and goodwill today through your power.

The Fringe of His Coat

by Mary Harker

"Daughter," he said to her, "your faith has made you well. Go in peace."

LUKE 8:48 (NLT)

THE DISORDER HAD imprisoned her for twelve long years. Stories of healing flooded in from all over. Her mind explored the possibilities. *Could he be the one to bring my healing? Does he have the answer to my dilemma? I have nothing to lose by going to him. And maybe, just maybe, if I can touch the fringe of his coat, I will be whole again after all these years.*

She bolted out the door, searching for the rabbi, the crowd directing the way. She pondered how to get to him without causing those around her to be "unclean." Unobserved by the crowd, she fell at his feet and reached out to touch the fringe of his coat. Immediately, the blood stopped flowing!

But wait. What was happening?!

He stopped and asked, "Who touched me?"

As she turned to flee, he caught her eye. With eyes directed to the ground, she whispered the whole story while the crowd listened. *Daughter*, he called her. When was the last time someone had addressed her with such love and gentleness? Faith had been rewarded as he proclaimed health and peace.

The story of the woman with the issue of blood has long been one of my favorites, and the fictional depiction above comes from pondering what her experience must have been like. I can imagine her shame and isolation for so many years, and then Jesus acknowledged and healed her.

An influential leader from the synagogue asked him to come and heal his daughter, yet Jesus stopped, called her out, and listened to her story. There was no shame or chastisement for reaching out. She was an outlier yet accepted and blessed with physical, emotional, social, and spiritual wholeness.

Beloved, do you need peace today? Do you wish to be whole, complete, and healed? Jesus is the Prince of Peace and is waiting for you to reach out and tell him your story and desire. Fall at his feet and talk with him. We can have his peace if we hang on to him, even by a thread.

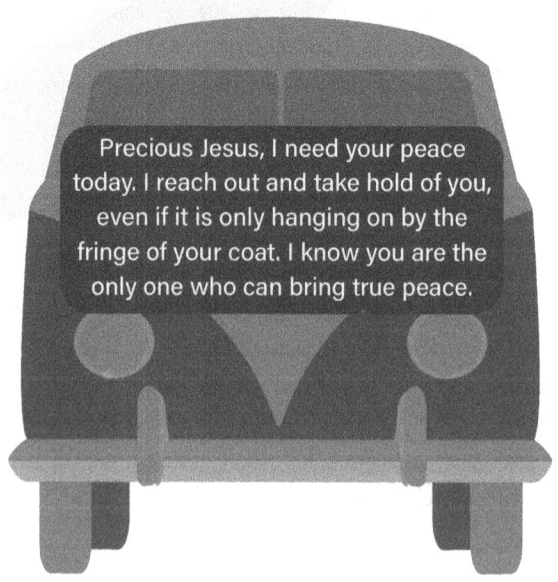

Precious Jesus, I need your peace today. I reach out and take hold of you, even if it is only hanging on by the fringe of your coat. I know you are the only one who can bring true peace.

Winds of Peace

by Becki James

Let me hear what God the LORD will speak,
for he will speak peace to his people.

PSALM 85:8 (ESV)

I DIDN'T WANT TO come back. But here I was again, eyeing the For Sale sign as I pulled into the driveway. I turned the doorknob, and my emotional meter spiked. It was the happiest place I'd ever called home. It should have felt like revisiting an old friend, but my guard was up. *Don't get all mushy, Becki. You're not staying.*

I spent months preparing my heart to leave this beloved place. Packing up memories in brown boxes. Staging shelves with treasures known only to our family. A large canvas I painted replaced the photo gallery wall. I stripped away every personal touch so potential buyers could envision themselves here. When all was picture-perfect, we loaded moving trucks and drove fourteen family members seven hundred miles south. I committed to this new adventure, looking for bright sides despite the deep internal ache. I detached every dangling thread that unraveled from my torn emotions.

Months passed. Buyers came and went. Offers fell through. And my positivity dwindled.

Now, I climbed the stairs to my bedroom and sat down at my writing desk. My hand swept away a light layer of dust. I gazed out the window into the woods below. The fall foliage spiraled down,

down, down. Tick. Tick. Tick. The droning clock hummed with nature. I paused.

The commotion of the past year seemed to rest on each leaf that floated silently to the grass. Red. Orange. Yellow. I felt myself exhale. A smile emerged. As autumn winds plucked leaves from their peak, God breathed winds of peace into me amid my own changing seasons.

Sometimes, I need to remember God's business is restoring his people. He desires an intimate relationship with us that quiets our spirits so we can hear him. After renovating three houses, traveling over four months as a professional basketball team chaplain, and sharing my home with fifteen people for an entire year, I needed the calm of his voice.

I found it in that moment. I realized living there was a beautiful season God gifted me, like a distinct peak of autumn. Coming back was also his blessing. He is with me always—waiting to speak peace on me. I need only seek him. He meets me with the splendor of his love and his tender mercy—the peace of my salvation.

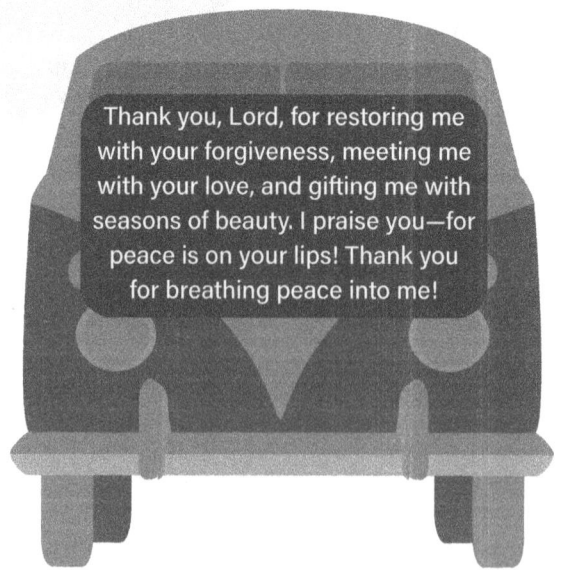

Thank you, Lord, for restoring me with your forgiveness, meeting me with your love, and gifting me with seasons of beauty. I praise you—for peace is on your lips! Thank you for breathing peace into me!

Our Miracle-Working Warrior

by Edna Earney

"The LORD will fight for you, and you shall hold your peace."

EXODUS 14:14 (NKJV)

HERE I WAS again, facing a sea of troubles and an onslaught of confusion, fear, and mind-bending weariness. The bills came in crushing waves. One toddler's cough grew harsher while the other two cried for attention. My husband was on the night shift and couldn't help, and I feared he would rather work than stay home with his sleep-deprived wife. I felt as if enemies surrounded me, ready for the final blow. I cried, just wanting a hole to crawl into.

Have you ever felt as I did, beleaguered and wishing for safety? Many of us have been there throughout history.

Consider Moses's Israelites when they saw Pharaoh's army approaching their camp. Pharaoh had freed them, then quickly reconsidered, and his armies pursued them to the banks of the Red Sea. The former slaves, surrounded by water and enemies, had no escape route. The Israelites first blamed their leader, but Moses encouraged them, saying, "Fear not, stand firm. And see the salvation of the LORD."[a] The Israelites cried for safety. How would God supply salvation?

Moses added, "The LORD will fight for you, and you shall hold your peace."[b]

a Exodus 14:13 (ESV)
b Exodus 14:14 (NKJV)

That old phrase "hold your peace" is an idiom meaning "be still or quiet."[7] In other words, "take the posture of peace" rather than shout anxiously at the leader. That was hard to do in their situation, with the enemy chariots racing and the Red Sea preventing escape! But Moses also gave them the source for their peace, their ability to stand firmly and quietly—God would fight for them. They wouldn't fight the soldiers, face annihilation, or find an escape route. They, instead, stood in peace and watched God's deliverance.

God indeed saved the Israelites by parting the Red Sea. A great east wind blew all night to dry the sand of the sea. The Israelites walked across dry land, and the sea swallowed the pursuing army. Because the Israelites stood quiet and still, they and the Egyptians witnessed God as the sole warrior and savior in Exodus 14. Both the victor and vanquished acknowledged God.

Even today, when we feel surrounded and in danger of being swallowed up, we go to the hand that parted the sea, our God who fights our battles for us. We can be at peace even in dire circumstances because God is our salvation.

Dear Lord, thank you for the miracles you work in our lives. We feel your love and find peace as you fight for us against our enemies. We give you all the glory as our warrior Savior.

Not Without You

by Joni Topper

Peace I leave with you, My peace I give to you; not as the world gives do I give to you. Let not your heart be troubled, neither let it be afraid.

JOHN 14:27 (NKJV)

"RODNEY FELL OFF our zip line and broke his arm." My sister called from the hospital eight hours from home, where my kids were visiting. "They wanted to keep him in the hospital overnight and do surgery to set his arm tomorrow. He said there was no way he would stay there overnight without his mom."

"What happened?" I asked my son over the phone.

"All the kids were riding the zip line. They just held on with their hands zipping across from tree to tree. I knew I couldn't hold on, but I didn't want to look like a weenie, so I did it too. I was right. I couldn't hold on that long just hanging by my hands. Mom, I'm not staying in this hospital without you."

When my sister returned to the phone, she let me know that he was so determined not to stay, the doctor agreed to set his arm while he was awake. She was appalled that he opted to endure the ordeal, fully aware.

"I could not watch. His bones are back in position, and we are headed back home. Rodney is ready for you to come get him. I doubt that he will sleep till you get here."

This incident is a distant, hazy memory now, but the power

of my son's insistence that I be there with him defines my reliance on God very well. Rodney did not care what he had to endure; he refused to be separated from the one who gave him peace. He trusted that my presence would offer him the assurance he needed.

Right then, only his mom could still his heart. I've lived through some moments when I felt the exact same way about my relationship with Christ. No one and no *thing* but Jesus could comfort me. When he speaks peace to my heart, I obey him just like a child. I am so thankful for his peace. The world simply offers no valid comfort for the many situations we face in life. I decided that being like a child who will settle for no one but their Comforter is a good thing. Just as I rushed to my little boy, my Savior sweeps in with comfort, giving me courage in the face of hardship with peace that's unexplainable. I pray people see my peace and recognize Jesus as the source.

Jesus, your promise of peace has carried me through many trials. Thank you for always being true to your Word.

Finding Peace and Purpose

by Mary Harker

Jesus said to them again, "Peace be with you. As the Father has sent me, even so I am sending you."

JOHN 20:21 (ESV)

BEFORE MY SON left for college, I felt the heavy burden of trying to reinforce essential lessons and principles for life. I made a book for his graduation with words of encouragement and blessings from significant teachers and mentors from his school years and made sure he packed it in his suitcases. The night before he left, with tears of bittersweet joy, I presented him with Scripture verses meant as a lamp and instruction, reminding him of who he was and whose he was.

I imagine Jesus felt that same burden preparing to leave his disciples. The scene in John 20, noted in the verse above, occurs on the evening of the resurrection. The disciples are huddled together in fear, hiding out behind locked doors. Jesus shows up among them and speaks words of reassurance and comfort. These particular words are a blessing of peace and purpose. Later, he promises to always be with them as he sends them out.[a]

When Jesus is in the room, there is peace. Walking with Jesus gives us the gift of freedom from fear and anxiety. His yoke is easy, and he gives us rest as we trek with him.[b] We don't need to hide, anticipating the worst.

a   Matthew 28:19–20
b   Matthew 11:28–30

What do we gain by staying close to the risen Savior? Below are three blessings to consider:

(1) We go from guilty to acquitted. Jesus paid the price for our sins and failures.

(2) We go from trembling to trust. Jesus gave his disciples the power to move in faith.

(3) We go from chaos to calm. When the scared disciples hid, Jesus gave them tranquility and courage amid the storm they faced.

After the blessing, Jesus sent his disciples out on a unique mission. The Father sent Jesus to bring us back to him. As believers and disciples, each of us has a part in sharing the good news of Jesus with others.

Amid our fears and uncertainty, Jesus gives us peace and purpose. When he enters our space, we experience wholeness and identity. We have the tools and skills to accomplish the tasks before us. In our weakness, he is strong.[a]

Jesus, thank you for giving me peace and purpose. I trust you to come through to supply for my needs. I'm grateful I don't do life alone but with you. You quiet my fears and empower me to accomplish your plans.

a   2 Corinthians 12:9

Finding True Peace

by Natasha Lynn Daniels

Don't worry about anything; instead, pray about everything. Tell God what you need, and thank him for all he has done. Then you will experience God's peace, which exceeds anything we can understand. His peace will guard your hearts and minds as you live in Christ Jesus.

PHILIPPIANS 4:6–7 (NLT)

AFTER SUFFERING THE storm of infertility and shattered dreams of motherhood for years, my husband and I received a call we'd been waiting for. A family chose us to adopt their baby boy. He was precious. He had blond hair, blue eyes, and the chunkiest legs I'd ever seen. Not long after sharing our news and celebrating with friends and family, we received another phone call letting us know that the parents started having second thoughts.

Despair gripped me, and my thoughts were filled with anger, questions, and worry about giving him back. However, the Lord gently reminded me of today's passage.

In that Scripture, Paul knew what it was like to suffer and seek true peace in the Lord. He encouraged the Philippians to pray and not worry while he was in prison for proclaiming Jesus. He knew what it meant to be content in whatever circumstance.[a]

a   Philippians 4:11

Finding peace for my situation that night on my own was not possible. I prayed and cried out to God, tears streaming down my face. Looking at that sweet sleeping baby in my arms, I thanked God for letting me be this baby's mommy for whatever time he allowed. As I prayed, his peace surrounded me. Even if I had to give back the baby, God was still good, and I would still praise him because I love God for who he is, not for what he gives me.

The peace that comes from the Lord is not the same peace the world gives. True peace is not found in the absence of suffering. True peace is found in trusting God through our suffering. It is the moment of trusting God that gives us the power of peace to face the challenges that will arise.

The Lord chose me to be Micah's mom. He is now a healthy, happy, know-it-all twenty-one-year-old. I know the ending doesn't always turn out that way. I have had many prayers answered differently than I hoped, but God is still good, and he is enough.

Lord, I give you my worries. Help me to trust you in every circumstance I face. I will worship you while I wait and know that true peace comes through suffering strong in you.

The Trail of Heart's Ease

by Lisa-Anne Wooldridge

Her ways are ways of pleasantness, and all her paths are peace.

PROVERBS 3:17 (ESV)

I SAT AT THE intersection for a long time, trying to follow the tiny squiggle on the map. I hoped it was an alternate route through the remote mountains—my planned path was flooded, the road washed away. I was on my own, researching a family story to write, in the days before GPS, smartphones, or, in my case, common sense.

"Which way should I go?"

I closed my eyes and reached for the comforting presence of the Holy Spirit. Every time I asked for wisdom, he answered, which was the only reason I'd made it this far.

Peace washed over me when I thought about turning to the right, so that's the way I chose.

"Oh wow. Oh, wow!"

Nearly coming out of my seatbelt with excitement because of the majestic view before me, I pulled off the road and onto the shoulder. I could barely believe my eyes—misty blue hills and emerald mountains bathed in golden rain-shine rolled all the way to the horizon.

The untroubled stillness of the mountains and the quiet music of the wind in the trees drew me further into a place of awe and rest. The beauty of that place seemed to sing a love song straight from the Father's heart. In the grass on the side of the road, a purple streak of heart's ease, a type of wild pansy, wound down the side of the mountain, surrounded by pink and white laurels and rhododendrons. My car followed the road to my destination, but my mind bounded down a different way, following the trail of heart's ease, the path of peace.

Peace led me to life-changing "chance" meetings and connected me with the spirit of wisdom. The absence of peace turned me away from danger and led me to safety. Peace gave me confidence and clarity along the way. I was chasing an old, ancestral story, but God was writing a new one in my life as I followed his peace. Where is his peace leading you today?

At every juncture in our lives, peace is always the way forward.

King of mountains and flowers, rain and sunshine, Lord of our paths and Prince of our peace, lead us in the everlasting way.

Peace on Earth

by Diana Leigh Matthews

And let the peace of Christ rule in your hearts, to which indeed you were called in one body. And be thankful.

COLOSSIANS 3:15 (ESV)

WHAT A TALL order! When I asked Mama what she'd like for Christmas, she responded, "Peace on earth." How could I ever provide that?

Later that afternoon, I took my grandmother shopping at a local department store. While perusing the aisles, I noticed an angel with gold wings. Mama always loved angels, so I stepped closer. My eyes widened as I read the inscription, "Peace on Earth."

Picking up the angel, I marveled at the nativity scene on a turning pedestal, the bodice of the sculpture. Mama had a collection of nativity scenes. Checking the price, I placed the angel back on the shelf and soon left the store.

Yet, that little angel refused to leave my mind. Once payday arrived, I was eager to return to the store. "Okay, Lord. If it's meant to be, that angel will still be there."

As I searched the shelves, my heart sank. I couldn't find it anywhere. Then I turned the corner. One angel remained.

I picked it up and ran my hand over the wood carving. With a turn of the handle, the music box began and played "Silent Night." Such a peaceful song.

Perfect! Just what Mama asked for.

On Christmas morning, as she opened her gift, I smiled. "I wasn't sure how we'd ever give you what you asked for, but God provided a way."

While we may long for peace on earth, there is one who can give us peace—the Lord Jesus. We just have to seek him and ask him. After all, peace is one of the fruit of the Spirit.

Sometimes, peace is hard to find in this troubled world. Yet, God whispers peace into our spirits. All we must do is ask.

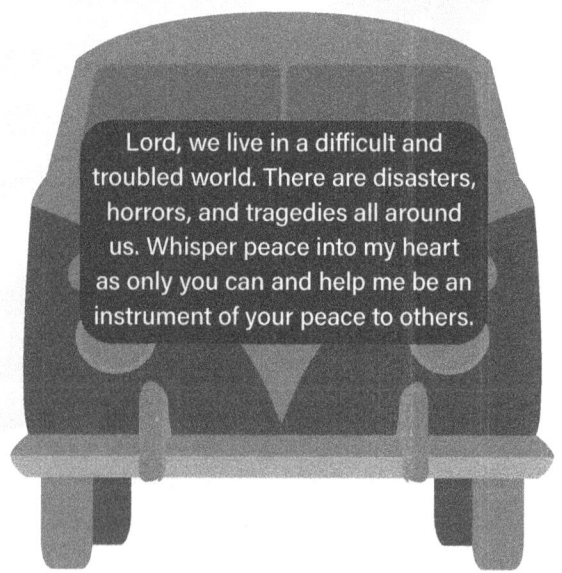

Lord, we live in a difficult and troubled world. There are disasters, horrors, and tragedies all around us. Whisper peace into my heart as only you can and help me be an instrument of your peace to others.

Trouble Sleeping?

by Robin Steinweg

In peace I will both lie down and sleep; for you alone, O LORD, make me dwell in safety.

PSALM 4:8 (ESV)

TOSS, TURN. TURN, toss. Inhale. Exhale. Sheep, sheep, no sleep.

What is the matter with me? I go through a checklist. I didn't have caffeine. I had fresh air and exercise. I ate healthy food. Drank plenty of water. Am I stressed? I don't think so. Well, there's always something that causes at least a little stress, right? But nothing major.

Why can't I sleep?

My friend commented that she sleeps easily and all night because she's a Christian and places her trust in God every day and night. So, God rewards her with the gift of sleep.

Great. What's wrong with me? I'm a Christian. I place my trust in God daily—and nightly too. Maybe I don't trust enough. Maybe my trust is weaker than hers. If I'm in Christ, shouldn't I be able to lie down and sleep because I trust God? Now, I'm not only anxious about an inability to sleep—I have guilt.

Toss, turn. Turn, toss. Inhale. Exhale. Sheep, sheep, no sleep.

And how will I function during tomorrow's busy schedule if I haven't had enough sleep? Will this lack of sleep erase years from my life? Will my granddaughter grow up without her grandma?

"I won't get to see her marry or enjoy my great-grandchildren," I whine.

When I have trouble sleeping, I sometimes pray or read my Bible. This time, I've turned to the book of Psalms. I'll start with number one and keep going until I'm sleepy. But when I come to Psalm 4:8, one phrase stands out: "I will both lie down and sleep." *Both?*

It's a wow moment. If I sleep, fine. If I lie down, I'm still resting. I can use this resting-while-awake time to simply *be*. I can pray, bringing others to my heavenly Father uninterrupted. I can worship through songs in my mind or silently repeat Bible verses I'd like to memorize. I can experience the refreshing, strength-giving joy of doing nothing except being in his presence. I can trust that he'll supply everything I need for what he assigns me to do tomorrow.

I can lie down in peace and sleep, and I can lie down in peace and rest. Both will refresh me.

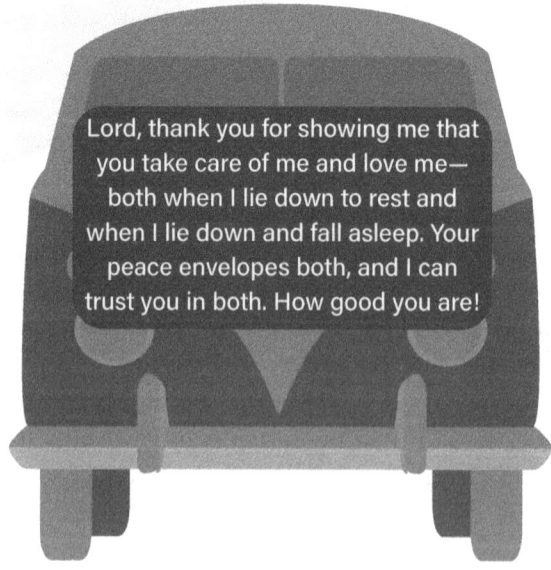

Lord, thank you for showing me that you take care of me and love me—both when I lie down to rest and when I lie down and fall asleep. Your peace envelopes both, and I can trust you in both. How good you are!

An Open Microphone of Peace

by Dixie McLeod

May God's peace and mercy be upon all who live by this principle, they are the new people of God.

GALATIANS 6:16 (NLT)

*W*HAT BEGAN AS a trip home to be with my mother during her recovery from a minor surgical procedure was ending here. Sitting in the quiet of the church sanctuary, beloved family and friends were waiting and remembering. We gathered on this October evening to honor my mother even as we said goodbye.

The minor surgery never happened. Instead, five hours after my plane landed, we were in the emergency room of a local hospital. Once admitted, my mother underwent multiple tests by specialists to determine what was causing her exhaustion and lack of appetite. Mother celebrated her eighty-seventh birthday in the hospital.

Visitors arrived, bringing dark chocolates, her favorite, as well as flowers and cards. The dreaded diagnosis of pancreatic cancer, stage four, also arrived. The cancer, already present in other organs, continued to metastasize. The words *terminal illness* seemed to ricochet around the room as if the message itself felt our pain and disbelief.

People rallied, sometimes weeping with us while they shared our shock. They comforted us with their presence and their words.

Words often punctuated with periods of silence, sometimes voiced in prayer, brought peace to circumstances in which peace would seem improbable, if not impossible.

The service celebrating my mother's life and legacy was beautiful. We commemorated a courageous life well-lived, a graceful life highlighted with humor. We knew, even if those gathered did not, what would occur after the last amen. The minister issued an invitation to anyone who wished to speak to do so via an open microphone. The room was silent, but only for a moment.

One by one, teenagers, octogenarians, her church family, and neighbors—those with whom she shared her life—came to the microphone. Everyone had a story to tell, a memory to share, a tribute to give. With each spoken word, sometimes coinciding with tears but often bringing laughter, came peace.

Peace, mercy, and grace filled the room and our hearts. God's peace, delivered to us by words spoken via an open mic, would be a gift opened repeatedly in the days and years to come.

Thank you, God, for giving us the ability to speak words, especially words that bring your peace. May peace always be the companion of the words I speak.

Promised Prayer

by Susan Stitch

*May God our Father and the Lord Jesus
Christ give you grace and peace.*

1 Corinthians 1:3 (NLT)

SOMETIMES, I LIE. A friend puts a request out on social media for prayer—be it an upcoming surgery, a problem with a relationship, or some other concern—and I quickly respond that I will pray for her. I even get specific, stating I will pray for peace, healing, wisdom, or some other highly desired result in a tough situation. While I have every intention of praying for intervention, I often forget. Thank goodness the Holy Spirit knows our hearts, and I desperately hope he takes requests heavenward!

In all but one of Paul's letters, he sought grace and peace for the recipients. While it was common for letters of the time to include a prayer or good wishes after the salutation, I believe Paul truly did pray for his readers as he wrote. Some of these letters went on to commend the readers; others included a firm rebuke and admonishment to change. Regardless of his intent, he usually led with this prayer for grace and peace. Most likely, Paul prayed immediately any time a need arose when he was with others. He must have realized God was eager to supply that grace and peace to anyone who made the request.

I, too, seek grace and peace for my friends and family. I want to actively pray for them whether they request it or not. When I forget, I let others down, and I definitely don't feel very peaceful. This awareness motivates me to pray while I respond. I'll turn my hopes for a good outcome into immediate requests for God's grace and peace—for others and myself. I'm so thankful for God's grace, and I desperately want the incomprehensible peace that only Jesus can give.

What would happen if we all added prayers of peace and grace to those who share their prayer requests with us? We can stop right where we are and pray for that!

Dear Jesus, thank you for your gifts of grace and peace. Please help me accept your grace and fill me with the peace that is beyond understanding.

God Calms the Storm

by Susanne Moore

For God is not a God of confusion but of peace.

1 CORINTHIANS 14:33 (ESV)

GRIPPED WITH A desire to worship but overcome with emotions of fear, shame, and uncertainty, I hesitated as I pulled open the door to a new church. I was immediately greeted by the pastor, whom I had met in my brother's hospital room. He was overjoyed to see me, and I felt welcome.

My brother was sitting by his drum set and waved as he got up to hug me. About four months prior, Chris had a heart attack and quintuple bypass surgery. I considered him a miracle walking. He was alive and worshiping God for the first time in many years. This brought me through the doors.

I personally had not stepped foot in a church in a few years. I was healing from experiences that had left me confused and ambivalent. Sparing you the details, I was grappling with my faith because people had hurt me deeply, leaving me vulnerable.

Something about worshiping God with a newfound freedom gives you a clearer perspective, though. God is the same always.[a] So, if God is not a God of confusion, as the verse above states, then someone else is, right? The author of obscure, hazy, or uncertain things is the opposite of truth. The one who lures us with deception is the enemy of our soul.

---

a   Hebrews 13:8

"Be sober-minded; be watchful. Your adversary the devil prowls around like a roaring lion, seeking someone to devour."[a]

I must be faithful to trust God when I experience those moments of hesitancy or lack of understanding. When I have that nervous stomach, could it be the Holy Spirit raising a red flag? Am I going to God's Word and finding out if what I see and hear is true, or is it a lie? People will never be perfect. We must rely only on the One who put the stars in the sky and sent his Son to die for us.

As I stood to sing well-known hymns that day back in church, I felt a calm sweep over my soul. My hands lifted naturally to the music and the beat of my brother's drumming. God resolves our struggle and lights our way forward. He does not confuse us; he calms the storms. If you feel perplexed, run to him with abandon and know he is always there for you.

> Heavenly Father, I come to you with a humble heart, needing your guidance. Help me lean into you, trusting you will never blur the truth or disorient my soul. You are the same yesterday, today, and forever. I put my hope and faith in you. When I'm feeling lost, baffled, or disconcerted, help me seek your truth.

---

a   1 Peter 5:8 (ESV)

Restoring Peace and Love

by Missy Eversole

Finally, brothers, rejoice. Aim for restoration, comfort one another, agree with one another, live in peace; and the God of love and peace will be with you.

2 CORINTHIANS 13:11 (ESV)

"HE IS GOING to fight you on this!" my husband warned me.

He was right, but this conversation with our sixteen-year-old son needed to happen. It would be a battle of wills, but I could tell my son was stressed and desperately needed rest.

As a junior in high school, Grant's schedule was filled to the max with advanced courses, after-school clubs, and play practice. He rarely got home until late evening, making late-night studying a new habit.

"I'm fine, Mom! I can do this!" he often proclaimed. He was right. He could do it. But at what cost? While our son was trying to do it all, the stress and anxiety were becoming unwelcome guests in his life and ours.

One particular week, on top of his regular already-packed routine, a standardized test was scheduled. Grant needed rest to perform well, and we felt it was in his best interest to miss a practice. He had only missed one play practice in his high school career. And that was due to *actual* sickness, not because he needed rest.

I entered the battlefield (aka our dining room) and found

Grant surrounded by his laptop, a pile of schoolbooks, and bottles of water to keep him hydrated and energized. Explaining that we thought it was wise to skip practice, I braced myself for the anticipated impact.

"No, I'll be fine. I have never missed practice because of a test, and I don't intend to now!"

"You don't understand what I'm saying. You are not going to practice," I insisted.

And with that statement, the battle had begun.

Our peaceful home erupted into a full-blown war of words. Grant wasn't happy with me. According to him, I was being unfair and overbearing. Words were flung from both sides, and eventually, my husband stepped in to calm us down and restore peace.

We live in a world where disagreements disrupt our peace. Let's remember to come together and love each other as God loves us. Grant skipped his practice to get some rest and received a high score on the test. Peace was restored, and joy returned to our home. We still reflect on that epic battle, but now it's filled with laughter and even the admittance that Mom was, in fact, right.

Lord, I've been wounded by someone's actions. Their words hurt my feelings. I know living in peace rather than strife with others is best. Please help me lead a restoration where we can once again live in peace with one another.

Will You Qualify?

by Beth Jennings Patch

Therefore, since we have been justified by faith, we have peace with God through our Lord Jesus Christ.

ROMANS 5:1 (ESV)

THE FAINT SQUEAK from my sneakers created the only sound in the dimly lit high school corridor leading to the gymnasium. My plan worked well. It was late afternoon, and everyone was gone. The bulletin board beside the gym doors held the list to my future. Did I make the team?

Last year, I came with friends to get the news. They were chosen and jubilant. I was not and couldn't get out of there quick enough to cry somewhere alone. I avoided repeating the chance of that experience with my calculated timing this year.

I stood directly in front of the list of cheerleaders for the upcoming year. I had practiced with my friends for weeks before tryouts. I knew I'd improved. However, my confidence did not exceed my painful memory because I came alone this year. My hope and anxiety were quickly replaced with disappointment, as my name did not appear with the others.

I would have made the team if eagerness, determination, and a great attitude were the criteria. However, they were not, and graceful movement with rhythm and good timing had evaded me since early childhood. I remember my mother's surprise when the teacher told her not to bring me back to dance class—my six-year-old, skinny legs got tangled up in the wrong direction every time I tried to pirouette. The cheerleading judges couldn't justify giving this awkward-moving teen a spot on the team.

Acceptance usually requires hard work, skill, connections, or other tangible characteristics. How comforting it is to know that God's acceptance isn't determined by these things. We can't do enough good things, help enough people, or give enough money away for God to accept us into his kingdom. (And a lack of those elements doesn't disqualify us.) Faith is the sole requirement—faith in his Son, Jesus Christ, as the one who paid the penalty for our sins with his life and conquered sin and death through his resurrection.

Such an all-encompassing truth floods our hearts with peace. We can approach the gates of heaven without worry. Through our faith in Jesus, our names appear on his list, the Lamb's Book of Life.

Father God, thank you for conquering anxiety and pouring calmness into our souls through faith in Jesus and the power of your Holy Spirit. Help me walk the corridors of my life overflowing with your divine peace.

The Peace–Piece Conundrum

by Hally J. Wells

So then, let us pursue [with enthusiasm] the things which make for peace and the building up of one another [things which lead to spiritual growth].

ROMANS 14:19 (AMP)

*I*F YOU WILL, consider two expressions regularly used in American culture. One phrase conveys a calm and sought-after state of being—it is *peace of mind*. Who among us doesn't desire that! The other—actually a noun—refers to an intangible thing used to act upon another person. For example, if I was angry about my bank's error, I might give the teller a *piece of my mind*.

Isn't it interesting that two similar-sounding expressions have such opposite meanings? The two really have no connection unless an individual gains peace of mind after giving another person a piece of *their* mind, and rarely does it work that way.

Today's world is full of contradictions when it comes to the idea of peace.

Exercises like meditation, mindfulness, and yoga are widely used to relieve stress, support focus and presence of mind, and improve overall wellbeing. Counselors and therapists teach young and old clients healthy coping skills. Walkers and runners, hungry for exercise and fresh air, flock to weekend 5K runs for a multitude of reasons and in all seasons. Healthy habits that fight frustration and foster contentment—these are all good things, right?

Unfortunately, we often behave in ways inconsistent with the inner peace we crave. We stream television shows that reflect anything but harmonious living. While we once watched programs about Christian families building their lives on midwestern prairies and namesake Virginia mountains, many now tune in to watch sons committing anarchy, lawyers trying to get away with murder, and housewives flipping over tables in rage. American teens play violent video games, and we offer kudos to public figures who verbally spar with aggression and without remorse.

Oh, that Satan! He sure does tempt us. Unwholesome books and movies, power-driven conflicts, competitions in our communities and on the world stage, and daily exhibitions of unchecked anger—they work on us.

While there's nothing wrong with watching a horror or action-packed flick or enjoying a feisty and worthy debate, perhaps we followers of Jesus might invest a bit more energy into the practices that never fail to bring us closer to peace. Meditating on his Word, stretching our prayer muscles, and communing regularly with other believers are great ways to find true peace of mind.

Almighty God, thank you for your Holy Word, the gift of prayer, and Christian brothers and sisters. Together, these quiet my anxious soul and help us live peacefully with one another.

Battling for Peace

by Robin Steinweg

Those who love your instructions have great peace and do not stumble.

PSALM 119:165 (NLT)

"I WANT YOU PREPARED. This could be ovarian cancer. The ultrasound looks suspicious."

These words from my specialist shook me. Surgery to remove at least one ovary would happen in three weeks.

Peace. It's a fruit of the Spirit. As a mature Christian, I should have plenty. But I confess, this scared me. Panicked me is more like it.

I'd had a few rodeos with fear, but nothing like this. Questions taunted. When I died, who would raise our teen sons? Would my husband cope? Oh, my poor parents.

Stop! *Stop it!*

How could I get peace? I'm a follower of Jesus. My heavenly Father loves me. His words promise *great* peace. That's not just any old peace. After all, I read, loved, and even memorized God's instructions—his Word.

I needed more ammunition. Fresh power that would help me in this fight. A peace-fight. There's an oxymoron for you.

Jesus fought temptation during extreme physical stress by speaking God's Word. That would be my strategy. I searched for verses. I must focus on Jesus because then I'd have perfect peace. After all, he's the Prince of Peace.

The Bible showed me peace could be a choice, and I could choose not to allow anxious thoughts to plant fear in me. In addition, I should be thankful.

Here's how it went: my stomach knotted, breath came shallow and fast. Fear attacked. I engaged. Armed with God's instructions, I met fear with truth, and the Prince of Peace himself fought for me, his presence winning every time. It took energy and determination, but he was faithful. I was thankful.

By the day of surgery, my fight for peace had grown easier. It was becoming habitual. Habits take less energy, so as I waited for biopsy results, the battle for peace wasn't nearly as intense. I felt ready to face the diagnosis of ovarian cancer.

The phone call came late one evening.

"I didn't want you to have to wait any longer," my surgeon said. "You do not have cancer."

Not every diagnosis has a simple ending like this. But perfect peace is possible when we follow the instructions of our King Jesus during battle. It can become our habit to appropriate his peace. He *is* peace.

Prince of Peace, King Jesus, I love your Word. I love you! Help me always choose to focus on you and your Word so I can experience perfect peace in any circumstance.

Road Trip

by Sally Ferguson

He came and preached peace to you who were afar off and to those who were near. For through Him we both have access by one Spirit to the Father.

Ephesians 2:17–18 (NKJV)

THE SNOW WAS blowing sideways, so I tightened my grip on the steering wheel. I'm always up for a road trip, but this one had me questioning my sanity. It's a six-hour round trip to the Pittsburgh airport from our spot on the atlas in Western New York, and winter driving can be dicey. But my beloved was on his way to Uganda, and I was tickled to share precious time with him on the way to the airport. Before getting out of the car, he assured me I had plenty of gas to get back to Erie. A quick hug and a kiss, and then he was gone. I plugged in the GPS on my phone and pulled into traffic.

There's a stretch of road between Grove City and Erie that is quite sparse. Open fields provide playgrounds for the wind and rain to mix into sleet and snow. That's where the gas light decided to come on. Shortly after, a sensor light began flashing. Their intermittent chatter beckoned for attention.

For some reason, panic never set in. Hubby said I would make it to Erie, and that was enough for me. As each barren exit passed, I reminded myself, "Roy said I can make it."

How often do I heed my Father's voice when life's warning lights go off? I have immediate access to God and his peace. As I remind myself of his promises, I can cling to the reassurance that he travels through life's journey with me. That is enough for me. Oh—and Roy was right. I made it!

> God, when my tank is near empty and warning lights from the stresses of life are going off, your presence provides peace. Why do they happen most when I'm away from the security of home? I thirst for you and nuzzle into your nearness. Fill my tank from your never-ending reserve today and empower me to settle into your peace.

With Peace as My Purpose

by Edna Earney

Walk . . . with all humility and gentleness, with patience, bearing with one another in love, eager to maintain the unity of the Spirit in the bond of peace.

EPHESIANS 4:2–3 (ESV)

*W*E'VE RECEIVED YOUR assessments, and we're happy to say you two agree on many criteria." This sentence of hope is one of the first things my husband and I say to couples in crisis. We mentor couples through Prepare/Enrich Ministry, a Christian program that gives couples tools to strengthen their relationships. When they hear their questionnaire indicated agreement on some points, I can see the surprise in their eyes because they've recently felt tension more often than harmony. With renewed hope, they enter mentorship a bit more at peace, a bit less defensive.

Isn't that true with most strained situations? If we find some points of common ground, establish that our goal is not to cause harm, and demonstrate a willingness to listen to the other's position, we'll find ourselves in a give-and-take conversation instead of a you-versus-me combative stance. How can I expect to change someone's opinion if she doesn't believe I've heard hers?

As Paul wrote to the Ephesians about unity among Christian believers, he didn't address any specific controversy. Rather, he created a portrait of the body of believers. In Ephesians 4, Paul describes one universal body, one Spirit, one hope, one Lord, one baptism, and one God over all as its head. It's hard to miss his steady repetition of the word *one* in two verses. As we interact with believers of different denominations, with the members of the church across the street, let's remember Paul's portrait of *one* and his instruction to walk with humility, gentleness, and love. We are not to compete or point fingers but be "eager to maintain the unity of the Spirit in the bond of peace."

If I purposefully walk in peace, reaching unity with others takes fewer steps. With peace as my goal, I'm more likely to be patient and bear with my spouse's annoyances. I'm more prone to humility, putting my co-worker's needs ahead of mine. I can embrace the diversity of all denominations of the church, more likely to till the common ground for good produce rather than dig at differences.

Peace on earth began with Jesus when he humbled himself to live among us, then die for us, as God willed. We can honor his example by choosing to live peaceably and in unity with fellow believers, looking to God as our head.

Dear God, I sometimes find it hard to live in peace with people who don't agree with me. I'd rather argue, but I know arguing bears nothing productive. Help me focus on your example and keep peace and unity as my goal.

Got You Covered

by Mary Harker

"For shoes, put on the peace that comes from the Good News so that you will be fully prepared."

Ephesians 6:15 (NLT)

"HE HAS TEN perfect fingers and toes!" my husband and I exclaimed to one another. We met our son for the first time and uncovered his tiny hands and feet. They were beautiful. Why are the newborn hands and feet one of the first things we examine and even kiss? Please tell me I'm not the only one who does this!

Feet play a significant role in Scripture, from walking to washing and everything in between. In the verse above from Ephesians, Paul includes the feet as essential for covering in preparation for spiritual warfare. They are shielded with the gospel of peace. Jesus shared and taught through parables about the kingdom of God during his time on earth. His kingdom is one of everlasting peace. Restoring peace between God and man was his signature story. That is our signature story as well.

Our path may lead to hostility rather than harmony. Jesus experienced conflict with the leaders of the synagogue and even misunderstanding among his own family. Yet he brought the message of peace wherever he went. If I am in a heated discussion with my husband, I must remember he is not my enemy. In those times,

I can speak words of peace and reconciliation, or I can escalate the conversation. I choose how I respond.

The shoes of peace are just one of the pieces of armor given to fight the Enemy and to stand firm. The armor of God also includes truth, righteousness, faith, assurance of salvation, and the Word of God. Picking up these battle-ready armaments and applying them gives us strength to face the challenges and communicates acceptance and grace to those we encounter daily.

As you put on your footwear to go out the door today, remember God's peace covers you. His peace that passes all understanding is with us as we encounter the day's challenges.[a] We take his gospel to a world that desperately needs it. Let's stand firm in his shoes of peace.

Father, thank you for the good news of peace that brings acceptance and grace. Please help me embrace that peace and pass it on to those I meet today.

---

a   Philippians 4:7

Who Wears the White Hat?

by Edna Earney

Deceit is in the heart of those who devise evil,
but those who plan peace have joy.

PROVERBS 12:20 (ESV)

*T*HE DASTARDLY VILLAIN slithered onto the stage at the local theater. "Hiss! Boooo!" shouted the audience, following instructions given to us before the curtain opened. Kiddos happily tossed handfuls of popcorn at the stage. Then, the pretty damsel in distress gained the spotlight, and the audience responded, "Awwww!"

A second spotlight spun toward the handsome hero in a white hat. "Hurray!" rang across the audience, full of smiles as the hero saved the damsel and all was right with the world.

That afternoon at the theater with my family was so much fun because the director planned the interactive responses and handed out bags of popcorn ready to be eaten or tossed at the villain. Don't we all love a good villain? It's fun to hiss and boo, knowing the good guy will save the day.

Real life is a bit different. We aren't assured the good guy will always win. Sometimes, we question which person is the villain and which is the hero. The dastardly villain on stage gives us so many clues: he wears black, grins at another's troubles as he twirls his mustache, and states his evil intentions aloud. Without those obvious signs, we don't find it easy to know a person's heart. Is deceit leading that person's actions, or is joy? If deceit, they will plan evil. If joy, they will plan peace. We aren't omniscient like our good God, so we must discern by observing, weighing the evidence, and asking the Holy Spirit for guidance.

Let me make this personal. I sometimes consider options for my behavior. Some options might come too close to the line of illegal, immoral, or unethical behavior. No one else knows, and the option causes no harm to anyone, so shouldn't I take the easy way, the profitable way, or the way that makes me happy? Here's the scale I need to weigh my decision on: am I acting from deceit or from God's joy in my heart? If I don't know, I need to pray for discernment. I want to wear the white hat!

Hebrews 5:14 (ESV) says, "Solid food is for the mature, for those who have their powers of discernment trained by constant practice to distinguish good from evil." Distinguishing the dastardly villains from the handsome heroes is easy. Discerning the motivations of our own hearts and those of others requires practice.

Dear Father, help your children see the good guys and the bad guys easily. Uncover wicked motivations, even in my own heart, that I might plan peace for myself and my neighbors. Remind us to weigh behavior on your scale.

Peace Brings Life and Health

by Carolyn Gaston

A calm and peaceful and tranquil heart is life and health to the body.

PROVERBS 14:30 (AMP)

WHO NEEDS A peaceful heart these days? I do! Who is searching for life and health? I surely am. Maybe we all have questions about how to have a calm and tranquil heart and would all like to experience that peace and tranquility inside. But how do we get there?

I know if I don't trust God, I worry, and if I worry, my heart is not calm—not at peace. Could trusting God be the trail to a tranquil heart? When I know that *I know* that God is in control and that he wants the best for me, I can rest in his plan. I can trust that he cares for me and is working for my good.

But when I'm in a dark place, it's hard to see his light. It's hard to wait for God to answer my prayer and heal my broken heart. Sometimes, in pain and suffering, it's easier to worry than trust. That's when I hunker down and dig deep into the promises in God's Word. Even when I don't see things changing, I can trust that God is with me and plants peace in my heart.

So, for me, peace is all about trust! How can I trust God even when I'm in the storm? In the fire? In the dark? In the pain? This acrostic helps me have a peaceful heart when I'm waiting for God to answer my prayer.

Pray in God's presence—declaring that he is with you.

Express your emotions to God—telling him exactly how you feel.

Accept that you can't fix everything—giving God full control of the situation.

Connect your joy to the promises of God—admitting that his timing is perfect.

Expect a miracle—believing God is working even when you don't see it.

In your dark moments, may these words bring you light, health, and peace.

Lord, you know I want life and health, so I ask you to grow my trust and fill my heart with your peace, even if I'm in a dark place. For I know you are always with me.

Peace in God's Presence

by Becki James

The LORD bless you and keep you; the LORD make his face to shine upon you and be gracious to you; the LORD lift up his countenance upon you and give you peace.

NUMBERS 6:24–26 (ESV)

"JUS WANNA SIT wiv you, Mimi. I wuv you."

Before I could speak my love in return, my grandson, Zach, climbed onto my lap, straightened his legs out over mine, and decided I was the comfy chair of choice. His grin radiated through his small body until I smiled from the inside out! With numerous family members gathered and other seating available, he picked my spot on the floor—with me.

What do you think makes God smile? What causes him to turn his face toward us with love? I cannot help but think of little Zach's eyes locking on mine with a twinkle of contentment, indicating he was exactly where he wanted to be. I wonder if I convey the same adoration when meeting with my Lord? And does God light up when I choose him over all else?

The Lord spoke to Moses with instructions for Aaron to bless the people of Israel. Within this blessing, God disclosed the secret to living without strife. Peace is not found in riches, power, or a life of solitude—God bestows peace through the blessing of his presence.

The Lord's presence in our lives is the greatest gift he gives us. Think about that on a personal level. *God chooses to be with me.* When I think about Zach's face zoning in on me from across the room and his running to be near me, I cannot help but compare it to my own relationship with the Lord. Do I drop everything and rush to my Lord's feet? Do I seek him with such passion? In a birthday party full of kids and toys, one child found something better—a place of love. I pick love.

I want to be completely content to rest in my heavenly Father's company. I want to sit there long enough and often enough to feel his face shine down on me. If I have his love, then I have his peace. And I think the next time I come before him, I will say, "I just want to sit with you, Lord. I love you."

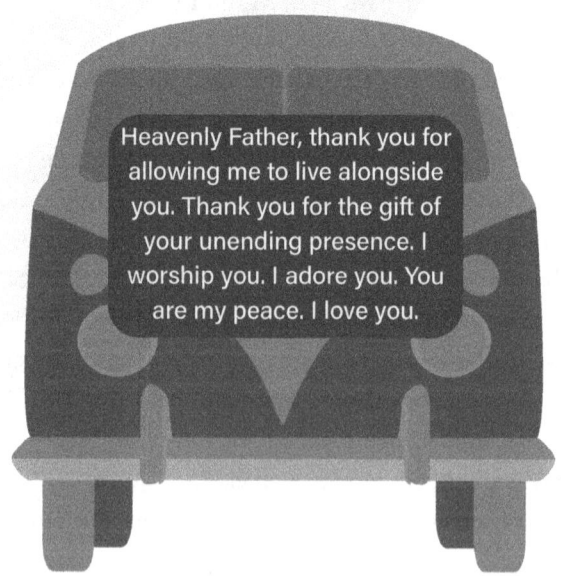

Heavenly Father, thank you for allowing me to live alongside you. Thank you for the gift of your unending presence. I worship you. I adore you. You are my peace. I love you.

Calm Instead of Chaos

by Kathy Carlton Willis

"I have told you all this so that you may have peace in me. Here on earth you will have many trials and sorrows. But take heart, because I have overcome the world."

JOHN 16:33 (NLT)

ON THE DAY of our move, it felt like I experienced every human emotion. In fact, the circumstances were so extreme that it triggered some PTSD. It was *chaos*, and I needed *calm*. I sensed God's presence, and he held me tight. We finally got everything loaded, including Hettie (our Boston terrier) and ourselves, and hit the road to our new destination. We were suddenly surrounded by a literal storm as we traveled (high winds, hail, torrential rains, most cars on the side of the road except ours and a few others). God nudged a friend to send me a text. But I didn't know it was her. (I didn't have her number in my contacts).

She texted, "Hey sweetie. How's the move going? Ya'll managing to dodge this weather?"

I knew from the area code that it was one of three people, so I felt safe texting and replied, "We're driving toward the storm."

She responded, "It's pretty rough, but it should pass quickly. Sunshine behind it. Hopefully and prayerfully, it will be past your place by the time you arrive."

She gave me the hope of perspective because she lived on the other side of the storm, and it had passed her place. She was already enjoying sunshine again. God blew me away by nudging her to reach out to me at the very time we were entering the storm. It was definitely a God thing. Mom gets as tense as I do during storms, and she was in the vehicle with us. I read the text aloud to her, and it helped calm her as well. We kept saying, "The sunshine is coming!"

I texted the phone number a few days later to confess I didn't have this friend in my contacts to recognize her identity, and I wanted to thank her properly for the text. She said it was Wendy, and I told her why the timing was so amazing.

It made me think of how God's Word is similar to that text during our emotional storms and hard times. It gives the perspective of being able to see past our storms and into the calm and peace he provides.[8]

O Peace Speaker, thank you for bringing calm to my chaos today. Help me to have the perspective of hope, informing my mind and heart how to feel.

Contributors

DENISE MARGARET ACKERMAN shares life lessons from her spiritual journey. Her heart-centered devotions seek to encourage readers in their own walk with the Lord. Denise has four stories that will appear in upcoming Guideposts books and is a contributing author in four WordGirls books. High school sweethearts married for fifty years, she and her husband, Jim, play pickleball to stay fit for their eight active grandchildren. Reach Denise at dackerman.0922@gmail.com or on Facebook.

MINDY CANTRELL resides in Texas with husband, Bill, and cat-child, Ramjet. Drawing from life experience, she lives her passion, ministering to ladies' groups and writing devotionals. Mindy also spends time in North Carolina with the other loves of her life: daughter, son-in-law, granddaughter, and five fur babies. Mindy is published in four previous WordGirls Collectives and can be found sharing hope and grace and her grief journey at mindycantrell.com.

NATASHA LYNN DANIELS is a Christian communicator, author, and founder of Hope in Every Season Ministries. Her purpose is to encourage women ready to find rest for their souls by falling into a season of surrender, laying it all at the feet of Jesus. Her words inspire women that we have hope in an unchanging God as we face changing seasons. Natasha's favorite titles are wife and mom. natashalynndaniels.com

EDNA EARNEY revels in life's diamonds uncovered from coal—our affirming, truth-revealing moments in life. She taps into such transformations so her readers see their own valuable treasures revealed in hard times. With her husband, Mike, Edna enjoys sharing God's vision for relationships as a Prepare/Enrich marriage mentor and trainer. Retired from teaching English, she has contributed to several WordGirls compilations and written her family history, *Weaving the Earney Tapestry*. Contact Edna on Facebook @TapIntoTransformation.

MISSY EVERSOLE loves living audaciously for Jesus. As an author, podcaster, and speaker, she encourages women to live out their love and faith for him with unwavering courage and conviction. She is living proof God will give you the boldness and courage to step out in faith. Missy resides with her husband and two adult sons in Morton, Illinois. Connect with her at missyeversole.com and at her *Bold Faith Now* podcast.

SALLY FERGUSON enjoys connecting with women and helping them find encouragement from God's Word. She is a retreat junkie and created a resource for planners at bit.ly/PlanRtWkbk. Sally lives in Western New York with her husband and her dad and is working on a Bible study for caregivers. Catch up with her at sallyferguson.net.

A retired teacher and administrator, **CAROLYN GASTON** now spends time threading words together and crafting rag rugs. She is a part-time ESL instructor and leads a ladies' Bible study through the small group ministry of her church. She loves camping, fishing, spending time with family, and baking for her ten grandchildren.

As an adoptive mom and author, **MARY HARKER** offers inspiration, support, and service to women navigating adoption. Her messages also provide truth, hope, freedom, and power to readers adopted into God's family. She is a contributing author in five devotionals and a guest contributor online. You can read more from Mary on Facebook at @maryjharkerreflects and Instagram @maryjharker or her website at maryjharker.com.

BECKI JAMES is an ally to all who desire to live in the presence of God. With an "old friend" flair, she gently guides hearts to the throne of God. Whether she's ministering with microphone or pen, Becki's way with words brings her audience into her storyline. She enjoys resting by the water, gathering at a table of friends, and loving on family. She and husband, Duane, call New York and South Carolina home. beckijames.com

BETH KIRKPATRICK is a wife, mom, and grandmother who enjoys reading books and laughing with her friends. She strives to be a light for Jesus by being a good listener and sharing encouragement with others. She is a contributing author in the books *Snapshots of Hope & Heart*, *Live & Learn*, and *Sage, Salt & Sunshine*. After many years of working with elementary students, Beth now works with adults in a literacy ministry. bethakirk@yahoo.com

SANDY LIPSKY tries to sit still and compose the things God whispers in her ear. During the day, she writes, teaches piano, and cares for her household. Nighttime finds her reading. Sandy is a contributing author to four WordGirls Collective books. Her most recent work can be found in *Renewed Christmas Blessings*, a Life Repurposed compilation. She enjoys Georgia's seasons and spending time with her husband, daughter, and playful dog babies Maple and Janie. sandylipsky.com

CHARLAINE MARTIN shows women how every day is an adventure with God. She and her Boaz love sharing tickle bugs with their grandchildren, cycling on Florida bike trails, and putzing the skies in their single-engine plane. She is an author in some of the WordGirls Collective series and a contributor in *Content Magazine*, online, and guest blog posts. She is also a speaker and Christian wellness coach. You can connect with her at charlainemartin.com.

DIANA LEAGH MATTHEWS shares God's love through her story from rebel to redeemed. Her day job is as a volunteer coordinator, but at night she writes and hunts genealogy. She gives programs as a speaker and teacher, and presents historical monologues. Leagh (pronounced Lee) is the author of *Carol of the Rooms, Forever Changed, 90 Breath Prayers for the Caregiver*, and others in the Breath Prayers series. She writes the history behind hymns at DianaLeaghMatthews.com

DIXIE McLEOD delights in sharing her passion for the study and teaching of God's Word. Often writing her own teaching materials, she also authors daily devotions for family and friends. Dixie is a retired vocational rehabilitation counselor with an MS in education with an emphasis in vocational rehabilitation counseling. For over fifty-five years, she's been married to husband, Tom. Their favorite activities include spending time with their children and four granddaughters.

JANICE METOT is, first and foremost, a mother of eight and Nana to eleven. She is now finding her voice as a writer. She serves in worship ministry at her church and has a lifetime of experience in nurturing, teaching, and encouraging others. She hopes her words provide strength and perspective and cause those who pass by along the way to stop and reflect for a while.

SUSANNE MOORE empowers women to grow in faith. She loves the redemption of her life in Jesus. She is a life coach, speaker, and author. Susanne is part of the Well Woman Alliance, supporting women seeking healing. Four of her pieces have appeared in prior WordGirls Collectives and she is a contributing author in *Radical Abundance*. She is currently writing a Bible study as well as her memoir. Home is Mansfield, Texas, and you can find her at susanne-moore.com.

BETH JENNINGS PATCH is a digital editor and writer at the Christian Broadcasting Network, where she manages the Faith section of CBN.com. She earned a master's degree in journalism from Regent University and a bachelor's in communication from the University of Virginia. Her passion for others to see God's goodness fuels her desire to write inspirational content.

Pondering and sharing the gospel through writing, speaking, and teaching is one of **BETTY PREDMORE'S** favorite things to do. She engages her audiences with her easy, conversational style. Betty has written three devotionals, *Pondering Virtue*, *Whispered Grace*, and *Ponderings of a Not-so-Super Mom*. She has contributed to numerous book compilations and written for Christian magazines and blogs. You can visit Betty on her ministry page at momsenseinc.org.

PATTIE REITZ is a proud Air Force chaplain's wife and mother of two adult daughters. With over twenty-five years of experience in education, she currently teaches composition at a local community college. Her writing is included in the books *Sage, Salt & Sunshine*, *God Strong*, and *Faith Deployed . . . Again*, and in the *Open Windows* periodical. She and her husband make their home wherever the Air Force sends them.

STACY SANCHEZ is a pastor, award-winning author, speaker, and business owner. Her articles, blogs, and books connect holiness to everyday messy life, from curveballs to communion. Stacy is an expert in grandparents raising their grandchildren and works to increase awareness and support for the cause. Learn more about Stacy at stacysanchez.com or on Facebook and Instagram.

JOANIE SHAWHAN shares true-life stories, offering her reader an eyewitness view of the action. Her Selah Awards finalist book, *In Her Shoes: Dancing in the Shadow of Cancer*, reflects the value of "your story plus my story become our stories." An ovarian cancer survivor and registered nurse, Joanie speaks to medical students in the Survivors Teaching Students program. She co-founded an ovarian cancer social group. For additional books and interviews, visit Joanie at joanieshawhan.com.

ROBIN STEINWEG writes, edits, and ghostwrites. She's a contributing author of the books *Sage, Salt & Sunshine*; *Wit, Whimsy & Wisdom*; *Live & Learn*; and *Snapshots of Hope & Heart*. Find her writing at *Keys for Kids*, and *Today's Christian Woman*. Read her daily prayers for parents and those with children in their lives at Prayerenting on Facebook and encounter bits of positivity with songs on her YouTube channel. Access both at robinsteinweg.com.

SUSAN STITCH enjoys looking for God in everyday situations and sharing his love with others. As an avid quilter and quilting instructor, she loves piecing together both fabric scraps and God's Word to offer warmth and love. Susan spent her career in corporate America and has been a speaker at women's events for the past twenty years. She's been married to her husband, Doug, for over forty years, and together, they have raised five children.

JONI TOPPER helps people see God's glory. She answers to many titles. Grandmother, speaker, worship leader, and author are some of her favorites. In 2023, Joni contributed stories to three books, wrote numerous published articles, was keynote speaker at a women's event, and guested on podcasts. Her memoir, *The Power of a Well-Placed Yes*, pulled from twenty-eight years as a pastor's wife, recently launched. Check her website for details and for speaking requests. morningloryministry.com

Inspired by people and personalities, retired school counselor **HALLY WELLS** writes and speaks about faith, parenting, and mental illness. A recent empty nester, Hally has three grown kids, who, along with many students, have awed and exhausted her in beautiful ways. Hally helps overwhelmed parents find practical answers, impactful resources, faith-family support, and divine wisdom—digging deep enough to find the good stuff, reaching high enough to find the best! Visit Hally at hallyjwells.com.

Known as God's Grin Gal (and the WordGirls' WordMama), **KATHY CARLTON WILLIS** writes and speaks with a balance of funny and faith, whimsy and wisdom. Over one thousand of Kathy's articles have been published, and she has several books in her Grin Gal brand. Her words inspire grin-worthy moments despite groan-worthy experiences. Check out her YouTube channel and sign up for Kathy's mailing list at kathycarltonwillis.com.

DAWN WILSON shares God's truth with clarity and love. She writes for Crosswalk.com, has co-authored two books, and is a contracted researcher for Revive Our Hearts, a women's Bible-teaching ministry. She blogs at *Truth Talk with Dawn*. Dawn is currently writing a book based on her struggle with multiple myeloma, while pointing women who hurt to hope in God's Word. Dawn resides in Southern California with her husband, Bob. dawnmariewilson.com

LISA-ANNE WOOLDRIDGE is inspired by illuminated manuscripts and stained-glass windows. Her heartwarming true stories have been published in several popular collections. Her second novel in The Cozy Cat Bookstore Mysteries, *The Rose and Crown*, is now available online. She lives in the land of mountains and valleys that drink in the rain of heaven—otherwise known as Oregon. You may find her at Lisa-Anne.net.

NOTES

1. Author unattributed, "I Can't Feel at Home Anymore," 1919, accessed March 11, 2024, https://hymnary.org/text/this_world_is_not_my_home_im_just_a.

2. Kathy Carlton Willis, *The Grin Gal's Guide to Joy: A Story, Study & Steps 7-Week Bible Study* (Beaumont, Texas: 3G Books, 2023), 106–108.

3. Sam Storms, *Pleasures Evermore: The Life-Changing Power of Enjoying God* (Carol Stream, Illinois: NavPress, 2000), 60.

4. Kathy Carlton Willis, *The Grin Gal's Guide to Peace: A Story, Study & Steps 7-Week Bible Study* (Tyler, Texas: 3G Books, 2023), 32–34.

5. John A. Witmer, "Romans," in *The Bible Knowledge Commentary: An Exposition of the Scriptures*, ed. J. F. Walvoord and R. B. Zuck, vol. 2 (Wheaton, Illinois: Victor Books, 1985), 496.

6. Don S. Armentrout and Robert Boak Slocum, eds, "Nunc Dimittis," *An Episcopal Dictionary of the Church* (New York: Church Publishing, 2020) accessed January 27, 2024, https://www.episcopalchurch.org/glossary/nunc-dimittis/.

7. *The Britannica Dictionary*, s.v. "speak your piece," and "hold your peace," accessed March 9, 2024, www.britannica.com/dictionary/eb/qa/speak-your-piece-and-hold-your-peace.

8. Kathy Carlton Willis, *The Grin Gal's Guide to Peace: A Story, Study & Steps 7-Week Bible Study* (Tyler, Texas: 3G Books, 2023), xiii–xiv.

Acknowledgments

This book was made possible due to some very special people. Named below are those who believed in the gift God placed inside of us. Thank you for the love, joy, and peace you've added to our lives. We want to acknowledge your support and help.

We have grateful gratitudes for:

Our buddy editors. Each devotion was edited by at least one buddy editor before the contributing author submitted the piece. Some received input from multiple buddies. We couldn't have done this project without you. In addition to the contributing authors helping one other (a beautiful thing to watch!), we benefited from feedback from Kristine Accola, Jessica Birdwell, Lori Lipsky, and Ellen Richards. Thank you for helping us out.

Our WordMama, Kathy Carlton Willis. You coordinated the project and shared ways for us to make improvements. We're grateful for your fine-tuning our devotions so they help our readers have a moment with God and his Word. Your patience in answering our questions and teaching us through the process will help us in the long run, even though we know you could have done it faster on your own. You have patterned God's love, joy, and peace for us. Thank you for caring enough to make sure we give our best.

Our families and friends. You cheered us on and managed without us so we could write. You continue to support our dreams and pray for God to use our words. You are the book's best team of influencers and launch celebrators! Every time you read and review our work, you help us succeed. *Love, Joy & Peace* is possible in part because of you. Thank you for affirming the gifts in us and encouraging us to use them as we write.

Our editor and book designer, Michelle Rayburn. Your artistic book cover design and interior design do such a great job of reflecting our WordGirls brand as well as our hearts. We are super excited about this cover! Your attention to detail with our edits made sure we followed industry standards. We are in awe of your creativity and work ethic. Because you strive for excellence, we can be proud to have our work included in a book that looks so professional. Thank you for our beautiful book!

Our churches. We value the fellowship of faith. Because of our heavenly Father, we are family. You give us local opportunities to express love, joy, and peace.

Our Lord. May this book bring you all the glory. It is because of you and your Word that we have words. You are our source of love, joy, and peace. Any version of these traits apart from you pales in comparison to what we have in you. We see it as a blessing to receive your direction as we write, and we are grateful for the opportunity to inspire others. What a privilege to be your WordGirls.

WordGirls Collective Books

WordGirls Collective Books
Our Essay Collectives

Sage, Salt & Sunshine

Introducing forty-eight life shapers and difference makers, and the traits that make them extraordinary women.

Sage, Salt & Sunshine features first-person stories about women who made a difference in this world. Allow the storytelling narratives and scenes to sweep you up into the lives of these exceptional women. Together we can figure out this life thing much better than trying to go it alone.

Who are our spiritual mothers? They are the ones who spent time with us when it wasn't convenient. Their lives patterned the life of Christ to us in a way we could emulate and pass on to the next generation. They didn't get everything right, but they showed love when we needed it most. They helped us fall in love with Jesus and made the Bible come alive to us. They not only helped us to grow spiritually, but they showed us practical, everyday ways of living life.

Our prayer is that *Sage, Salt & Sunshine* will motivate you to show gratitude to your spiritual mother and inspire you to be a life-changing influence on other women watching you.

Live & Learn

When we say, "Well, live and learn!" we think of surprising outcomes.

You'll relate to these essays if you're tired of figuring out God's guidance the hard way. *Live & Learn* features first-person stories about unexpected lessons from twenty-seven WordGirls. God uses big and small circumstances for monumental life-transforming moments. Even the insignificant can make a big impact when we pay attention.

The expression "live and learn" has been passed down through time to mean we often grasp life best by experience. Some of us catch on the hard way or take multiple times to comprehend and apply this sort of training.

Come discover the unexpected with us as you read along about: Childhood life schooling, hilarious ahas! with ha-has, embarrassment as a teacher, turning points in life, stranger-than-life teachers, and tough-but-tender love.

You will find these essays to be a balance of funny and serious, dialogue and narration, weighty and light.

Our prayer is that *Live & Learn* will help you have your own studies in God's classroom. Be on the lookout. It just might happen when you least expect it!

Our Devotionals

Snapshots of Hope & Heart

When we hear the word snapshots . . . we think moments.

In this WordGirls Collective, we researched what God's Word says about the topics of hope and heart. *Snapshots of Hope & Heart* includes eighty-four devotions written by thirty-four WordGirls.

The authors inserted stories, much like snapshots, to help us capture a true-to-life inspirational insight fitting for the daily Scripture. We hope the takeaways will stick with you throughout the day, similar to the memory of a snapshot long after you've tucked it away.

Enjoy taking a moment with God as you read this devotional. Take your own snapshots as you look through our album of hope and heart.

Our prayer is that these words will deliver word pictures of hope and heart to save to your mind's photo album. In that frame of reference, the Bible is the faith family album deserving to be passed down through the generations.

Wit, Whimsy & Wisdom

Seeking special time with God each day?

Wit, Whimsy & Wisdom is here to be your guide. In each devotion, look for a concept you can refer back to in your thoughts as you go about your day. The stories will give you some grins, some grace, and some grit to help you through the struggles you face, as well as help you celebrate moments of victory.

This three-month devotional is divided into five relevant sections. Feel free to read it straight through or choose what you need that day. Our sections feature Worship & Prayer, Humor, Family, Spiritual Growth, and Women's Issues.

Wit, Whimsy & Wisdom was the first WordGirls devotional, designed to use God's Word and the words of WordGirls to help you fall in love even more with the Word made flesh—Jesus.

Our desire is for you to find nuggets within these pages that make you think, inspire you to worship, and even give you a few laughs along the way.

www.ingramcontent.com/pod-product-compliance
Lightning Source LLC
Chambersburg PA
CBHW070143100426
42743CB00013B/2810